Winning Secrets No One Tells New Real Estate Agents

How to Go Solo Without Going Broke

By

E. Theodore Aranda

ISBN-13: 978-1544623528 (CreateSpace-Assigned)

ISBN-10: 1544623526

BISAC: Business & Economics / Consulting

DOWNLOAD THE AUDIOBOOK FREE!

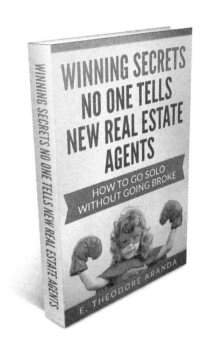

READ THIS FIRST

To Thank YOU,

I'd like to give you the Audiobook version 100% Free!

To Download go to: http://etaranda.com/downloads/

Dedication and Acknowledgements

This book is dedicated to my Father, who
will always be my True North. He is wisdom
in its purest form.

**I am deeply grateful to all the people who have made this book a
reality:**

Editors: Elizabeth Marks, Emeline Wilkins, & Sharon Odegaard

Audiobook: Scott Coyle

Book Formatting & Consultant: Elizabeth Marks

Angie Weeks, Mary Melendez, Jen Lukas, Becca Berlinsky,

Jonette Burke, Jack Tsai, Jessie Hesieh, Teresa Mendoza...

Rob Gowing, Myrna Gowing, Lynzy Gowing, Matt Odegaard, Bethany
Odegaard, Laurelle Gowing Brown, Debby Ferrarelli, Gina Robertson
Smith, Marian Kim-Phelps, David Phelps, Treesi Coyle, Marissa
Cornish, Mike Cornish, Shelley Smith, Valeri Wilson, Dale Huntington,
Ashley Huntington, Bill Krehbiel, Carol Krehbiel, Carmen Aratea,
Amber Clasen, Ann Carillo, Jordan Francis, Mario Castillo, Tom
Larson, Henry Ramirez, Kathi Ramirez, Megan Weber, John Day,
Annie Day, Sean Anderson, Sheryl McKay...

Joshua Boswell, Rob Scott, Brian Tracy,

Chandler Bolt, Dane Maxwell, Juliana Garcia, Josh Isaac, Caleb
Hodges, Kristen Guy, Anna Fitter, Mona Mordoff

...to you all and many, many others, I offer my sincerest thanks.

CONTENTS

Introduction: How You Can Beat the Odds 1

Section I: Why Most Agents Fail and What to Do About It............9

Chapter 1: Three Reasons Most Agents Fail................................10

Chapter 2: Your Superpower 15

Chapter 3: What Would You Do If You Could Not Fail?.................32

Section I Summary..42

Section II: The Secrets of Successful Agents 43

Chapter 4: The Fastest Path to a Steady Income.........................44

Chapter 5: Try This Instant Career Booster 55

Chapter 6: The Benefit of Doing the Right Thing Even When It
Hurts 65

Chapter 7: Give and Grow Rich..73

Chapter 8: What The Real Estate Exam Didn't Teach You
About Prospecting...79

Chapter 9: Learn This Skill to Bring in the Cash 87

Section II Summary 95

Section III: Will These Principles Work for You?......................97

Chapter 10: Three Simple Things You Can Do to Launch
Your Career 98

Chapter 11: Discover Your Unique Genius 105

ABOUT THE AUTHOR..112

Personal Note 113

Introduction

How You Can Beat the Odds

According to Trulia, 75% or more of New Agents fail and quit in their first year.

This troubled me.

So many new licensees start with big hopes and dreams and put a lot at risk, but they can't make enough money to stay in their new career.

Numerous failed attempts and setbacks force them to quit too soon.

While the creditors line up, financial pressures cause New Agents to buckle and collapse.

So they give up on their dreams and fall back on the same unfulfilling and soul-sucking job they did before going into real estate.

A real estate license alone doesn't bring in the income

I hope I've caught you before you've decided to quit.

Maybe you're thinking about quitting because you've overspent on your budget, failed to find clients, and lost the will to fight.

I have news for you: All the Top Agents have failed, too.

- Some of their best-laid plans crashed and burned.
- They suffered costly marketing efforts with dismal results.

1

- They've felt abandoned, confused, and mixed with self-doubt.
- Many Top Agents have been broke. More than once. Just like you.

The truth is that all of those failures are external symptoms of a deeper internal problem.

I set out to find out why

So I pursued the answers to three fundamental questions:

1. Why do some agents make it, while most fail?

Two agents can sit under the same trainers with the same material. One agent explodes with success, while the other quits.

2. What are the traits of successful agents?

What do they do when they're tempted to quit?

3. Can YOU acquire the traits of a successful agent and apply them for your own success?

Do successful agents have something you don't have?

Winning secrets revealed by top agents

For almost a year, I interviewed real estate agents at different stages in their careers, ranging from first-year rookies to top-producing veterans.

I discovered that none of them had extraordinary abilities or a secret formula that propelled them to success.

Rather, the Top Agents learned a handful of simple, powerful principles and mastered them with consistent practice. Each year they expanded their client base and increased their income.

They worked hard on the *right* things at the *right* time.

Now you can learn these principles and build a rewarding and lucrative career in real estate.

You can learn how to handle success and failure, overcome obstacles, and plan each day for productivity to make consistent sales like a Top Agent.

No special skills are required – just a willingness to learn and take action.

The real working-world information on how to build a successful business comes from the people who've done it. This is not classroom theory.

These are the core, common principles for success, straight from the mouths of the people who've succeeded.

This book contains more than 276 years of combined, professional real estate experience

My interviews with Top Agents (defined as those with incomes of well over $150,000 per year) revealed that a healthy mindset and productive daily activities are the core principles that shot them to the top within their first six months, regardless of market conditions. Cultivating these principles proved common to all successful agents.

You can achieve and enjoy the career you desire by following these same core principles.

Implementing these principles will:

- Enable you to succeed in the money-making aspects of the business – mindset and marketing.
- Help you overcome self-doubt and destroy self-sabotaging behavior by eliminating limiting beliefs.
- Reprogram your mindset with empowering beliefs so you can pursue and achieve the lifestyle and career you desire.
- Do fewer things with better results every day. Change your concept of time to boost your productivity and income.
- Bolster your confidence, so you can walk into a room full of strangers and leave with a notebook full of potential clients.

- Empower you to do the right thing, even when it hurts.
- Build an effective support team that will accelerate your progress toward success.
- Wield the power of generosity by "paying it forward." Create a lasting, global impact for you and your family.
- Introduce you to the one skill that can triple your income and shape you into the agent of choice.
- Discover your unique marketing genius.

These easy-to-grasp principles produce fast, long lasting results, and promise a prosperous career as you master them over a lifetime.

These principles may seem simple and obvious. But those who have ignored these principles have quit long ago with a bucket full of excuses and lost dreams.

Achieving success is not a complicated thing.

It may not be easy, but it's not complicated. By taking action and applying these simple principles, you'll unlock their real power and make it work for you. Put them into practice, and you'll enjoy the same success in life and business that generations of agents have enjoyed.

The benefits of putting the principles into practice

Once you discover what Top Agents do for a successful real estate career, you'll want to put into practice what you know. Even with all the best material set before you, only one thing will set you apart from all others: You must take action.

Don't be the person who dies a slow death in a job you hate, never being paid what you're truly worth.

Instead, you can be the person who makes everyone else wonder:

- Why you always seem to be on vacation
- Why you never answer to a boss
- How you're always home for your kids

- How you can afford to drive the nicer cars and live in the better neighborhoods
- Why you can *honestly* say you love your job.

Be the person who takes the chance to change careers for a lifetime of freedom and fulfillment.

How this book can be useful to you

If you're a New Agent, read this book before you begin. Doing so could save you a lot of time and trouble. Each chapter discusses the essentials of building a successful real estate business.

You never again have to feel like you've been thrown into the shark tank and abandoned to fend for yourself. No more guessing on what you need to do. You'll have the clarity and confidence to move forward, and you'll know how to ask for help when you need it.

As you grow in your career, use this as a reference guide and revisit it often.

This book will help you form the foundation for a healthy and prosperous real estate business.

And more importantly, a happier you.

If you're thinking of quitting because you're feeling beat up, overwhelmed, or lost in the woods, use this book as a place to pause and begin again. Sometimes, we all need a fresh perspective to help us refocus our efforts and regain our momentum. It is my hope you'll find the encouragement and practical wisdom you need to move forward with clarity in whatever you decide to do next.

Success is better caught than taught

You become the company you keep.

Hang out with successful people, and eventually you pick up on their mindset, values, and the habits that propel them to success.

This book is the next best thing to hanging out with successful people.

So do both: Bring this book with you when you hang out with Top Agents.

When you discuss these concepts with your fellow agents, you can accelerate your progress toward mastering these principles for a healthy business.

Make it a point to stay in good company with people who understand you and support your efforts toward your career in real estate.

If you imitate the way Top Agents think, and do what they do, you can build a lucrative career in real estate that rivals most doctors and lawyers in far less time than it takes to pass medical school – with a lot less effort, even if you dropped out of school. Some of the Top Agents I interviewed didn't have a college degree.

Top Agents vs Top Producers

You will read about Top Agents frequently throughout this book, so let's define WHO I mean by "Top Agent."

A Top Agent isn't necessarily a Top Producer.

Money is only a measurement of progress and achievement, not an end in itself.

Money only reveals how you used your time. Because, as a real estate start-up, your new job is to convert time into money.

A Top Agent possesses an enriching and financially secure lifestyle because of integrity as a real estate professional.

Three core areas to cultivate

This book explores common aspects of a Top Agent. How they cultivate their mindset and relationships with time, money, and people sharply distinguishes them from all others.

The focus of a Top Agent, rather than money, is on consistent self-improvement in these essential areas:

- Time management
- Money management
- Interpersonal relationships

When you master these three core areas, the income will naturally follow. Mastering each one is critical if you want a career full of purpose and meaning.

Many of the Top Agents interviewed run six-figure businesses only because they demonstrated mastery in the core areas. They made fundamental changes to their mindset and daily routines, and they took action on what they learned. They practiced the right things, and through the process, they transform their character, values, and perspective.

This is ultimately about your quality of life, not quantity of dollars. Pursue a quality of life, and the dollars will follow. Strive to be a Top Agent, and you'll naturally become a Top Producer.

Read what you need

The chapters in this book are in no particular order, so jump in and start reading whatever is most important to you.

If a chapter isn't relevant to you at the moment, then skip it and revisit it when it applies to you.

Of course, the best way is to read the entire book to get a good overview.

Each chapter is filled with solid, field-tested concepts, and practical advice from Top Agents.

You'll find suggestions on how to strengthen one or more of the three core areas in each chapter.

You can put practical suggestions to work for you immediately.

Chapter 1 sets out the top <u>three reasons most agents fail</u>.

Chapter 2 reveals how <u>Top Agents turn failure into success.</u> It all begins between your ears.

Chapter 3 is about <u>life without limits.</u> Confidence knows no borders.

Chapter 4 helps you <u>establish good daily habits for success.</u> Your habits are what got you here today. New habits will shape your tomorrow.

Chapter 5 will put you on <u>the fast track to a successful career.</u>

Chapter 6 empowers you to <u>do the right thing even when it hurts.</u>

Chapter 7 inspires you to <u>give and grow rich.</u>

Chapter 8 highlights the <u>money-making skills of</u> Top Agents.

Chapter 9 focuses on how to develop the <u>art of negotiation</u> to put more cash in your pocket.

This book won't overwhelm you with a ton of information, tricks, hacks, or strategies.

There are no secret formulas or magic bullets.

But, this isn't about finding the magic bullet.

It's about BEING the magic bullet in any office, at any time, in any town across the nation.

Here's to you and the new life you're creating today. Here's to the future you!

Read on to start now!

Section I

Why Most Agents Fail and What to Do About It

Ten agents will start under the same trainer, and learn the same material.

Eight will quit, while two will succeed.

Find out why, and learn how you can rewire your brain for success.

Chapter 1

Three Reasons Most Agents Fail

The deal was collapsing.

Tim paced back and forth in front his seller's house – his cheeks fire red, beads of sweat on his forehead, and his stomach churning. Glued to his phone, he was desperately trying to reach a plumber. Water seeped through the front door, onto the porch, and down the front steps from the house.

Today is showing day – and the buyers are not amused.

Tim was desperately counting on closing this deal.

For too long, he's been living just one big bill away from financial catastrophe. Visa, MasterCard, and American Express are sending nasty letters about collection agencies. The bank wants to repossess his car, while the medical bills, house repair bills, and utility bills are piling up.

And he has no clue how to tell his parents that he can't pay them the money he borrowed to cover last month's mortgage. Again.

After eight months, he has yet to close his first escrow.

Later today, he'll have to face his wife and admit that he lost another one.

He works hard to provide a safe and secure home. His wife's happiness is all he cares about.

But he fears he can't live up to everything she needs him to be.

She doesn't really know what's going on. Tim is always so distant and preoccupied. He rarely talks about the stress he's under. And his kids walk on eggshells, because they never know when he's going to snap at them.

Today he fears his wife will condemn him with blistering scorn for putting all the family funds at risk.

Tim feels alone in his failures.

No one understands what he's going through, and he doesn't know who he can talk to.

But to quit now would kill his dreams.

Tim is aching for a break.

If he could just figure out what he's doing wrong, maybe he'd have a chance to turn this around.

The frustrating thing is that he's done everything right: keeping daily notes, farming campaigns, cold calling, door knocking, door drops, blogging every day, updating his website, working his sphere, networking and camping at all the open houses he can get.

He's done everything they've told him to do in all the training and sales seminars.

Maybe you've had days, weeks, or months like Tim. Sometimes, it feels like you're missing something.

After multiple setbacks, frustrations, failures, and evaporating funds, you doubt you can really do this. You're ready to quit, give up on your dreams, and go back to that old soul-sucking job you had before.

Interviews with Top Agents reveal that Tim's setbacks, frustrations, and repeated failures are only symptoms of a deeper, invisible problem.

If 75% or more fail, how did the other 25% make it in the real estate industry?

What is Tim missing? What do Top Agents know that Tim doesn't know?

Are they smarter and more talented? Do they know special tricks and tools?

Do they have a magic bullet?

Nope.

Actually, Tim, you, and other New Agents can be just as smart and clever as those Top Agents.

And new tricks and tools can be fleeting trends. You don't need a magic bullet.

Magic bullets are myths.

It's true that two New Agents can start in the same office and train under the same coaches who teach all the same material. One agent will start making sales overnight, while the other will languish for months without a sale, until he finally quits.

Why does that happen?

First, let's look at what pushes New Agents to the point of giving up.

Three real reasons New Agents quit

A lot of New Agents shared with me why they quit. Three reasons surfaced.

1. They run out of money.

Most New Agents quit too soon because their money ran out on marketing expenses and because of poor spending habits.

At the start, they jump in and approach marketing backwards. Instead of focusing their efforts on a smaller market, they cast a wide net and try to be all things to all people. They broadcast to everyone using expensive marketing tools and methods. But they're only doing what they were told because that's how they were "trained."

When their money runs dangerously low, they rely on their poor budgeting skills to manage a personal financial crisis. Had they set good money habits early on, they could have avoided tragedy.

2. They lose their vision.

Dreams fade quickly.

Few New Agents take time to feed their life's vision every day through reflection and introspection. Without the daily discipline of reflection, they lose sight of their main goal.

Distractions in life overpower them until their dreams evaporate into a fog.

Lack of clarity is a motivation killer. Without a clear vision of what you want, every roadblock and setback becomes a reason to quit. As your vision fades, your passion fades along with your dreams. High hopes and good feelings will only get you so far.

Top Agents draw up "blueprints" for their success and review them each month.

It's just like building a house. Blueprints keep you on track – but more importantly, they help you *visualize* your future.

3. They function on limited beliefs.

A big reason New Agents quit too soon is because of Head Trash.

Head Trash is all your limiting and false beliefs about yourself.

Almost all New Agents lose at the Inner Game of Entrepreneurship, and they succumb to their negative self-talk.

Head Trash erodes your confidence, and triggers self-sabotaging behaviors like procrastination (failing to take appropriate action when it matters most), isolationism (refusing to ask for help), and defensiveness (fear-based alibis).

Unresolved Head Trash is the invisible reason most New Agents freeze and eventually quit.

Did you notice that two of the three reasons concern the way an agent **thinks**?

The truth is that Top Agents **think differently** from everyone else. They respond to success and failure differently. They consistently practice habits that train them for success.

Most importantly, they take action – even if it's not always the right action at first.

They fail fast, learn fast, and improve at lightning speed.

As a result, Top Agents learned how to handle success and failure.

They can make money when the market is up or down.

And they know how to build a business anywhere they go, in any market.

All the Top Agents said the same thing: If they can do it, so can you!

Your mind is a God given gift, and a limitless resource.

You can train yourself to think like a Top Agent.

Since you're gifted with the ability learn, you have the power to change your future.

Top Agent Success Principle: Think differently; train your mind for success

Read the next chapter to discover the most powerful thing about you.

Chapter 2

Your Superpower

Back to Tim.

He's doing all the hard work of an agent, but he has yet to make a sale.

For months, we were all worried about Tim. He's had dozens of opportunities to quit for very good reasons. So we waited for him to give up and do something else.

I asked Tim if he would feel better or worse if he quit today.

He asked why.

I told him that if he thinks he would feel better *after* he quit, then he's not cut out to be an agent.

But if he thinks he would feel worse, then it's good sign he should keep going.

"Okay...?" The tone in his voice wanted to hear more.

"Tim, you've been at this for almost a year, and you still haven't made a sale."

"I know..."

"You haven't even closed your first escrow. Without paying customers, you're not really in business."

"...Right." He looked away, distant and pensive.

"Then why continue?" I asked.

Silence. Then a long sigh.

"Because every time I've thought about quitting, I knew I would regret it."

I asked why.

Tim sat up and looked me in the eyes.

"Because I *believe* it's my calling."

No one can take that away from Tim.

He believes deeply that he's meant to be an agent, even when everything fights against him.

True to the stats, eight out of his 10 friends have already quit real estate.

But not Tim.

You might think he's foolish, but Tim has a superpower.

It can't be taken from him, and he has the right to exercise it when he chooses.

He's resisted the external pressures to quit because of this invisible force.

What is this invisible force?

Belief.

What you believe is the most powerful thing about you.

It determines the choices you make every day.

It controls your behavior.

Beliefs tell you what to love and what to fear. Your beliefs define who you are, and what you do.

When you're under the crushing weight of imminent failure, your beliefs empower you to press on when everyone else has given up.

We've all heard of Thomas Edison and his ten thousand failures.

But it wasn't mere determination that led him to success. It was a powerful, invisible force hidden below the surface.

It was Edison's *beliefs*.

He *believed* that there was a better way to make light. His deep belief woke him up on mornings when everyone else quit and slept in. His beliefs fueled his determination and patience.

The Wright Brothers were out brained and grossly underfunded in the race to conquer the skies.

But when they chose to exercise their invisible power, they defied the odds, the doubters, and financial challenges.

Orville and Wilbur *believed* there was a better way to fly.

When all others around them quit, their beliefs pushed them forward to make the first manned flight.

And today, we're free from the limits of gravity.

Alan Turing, the WWII cryptographer, believed he could beat the German Enigma Machine when everyone else thought it was impossible to crack encoded messages with 159 million million million possibilities. Turing believed only a machine could beat another machine.

It was the solution no one else thought of. Turing's deep *beliefs* drove him to ask for the audacious sum of $100,000 directly from Winston Churchill to build it. As a result, Turing built what we now know today as the first computer.

Turing was armed with more than determination. He was *fueled* by his deep beliefs.

A powerfully held belief will pull you toward your goals, not push you.

It destroys the barriers blocking your way, and it brings clarity to everything you do.

Never underestimate the power of your beliefs.

The belief and faith I am speaking of here is not necessarily religious.

Rather, it is the belief and faith we practice every day.

For example, we exercise our faith every time we travel on an airplane. Often, we've never met the pilot, and we don't know all the details of how an airplane works. Yet we jump on in faith, trusting that the plane will fly and the pilot will safely deliver us to our destination.

In that way, we exercise belief and faith every day.

We plan our days believing the sun will rise tomorrow.

If you're sitting in a chair, you're exercising *faith* the chair will support your weight.

The inner game of an entrepreneur

Our friend Tim believes he is called to be a real estate agent.

But he's doubting that right now because of all the failures and challenges. It's making him doubt his abilities. He feels he's failed everyone's expectations. He's carrying tremendous guilt over squandering the family's resources.

If you're like Tim, and you're feeling like you've lost your way...

questioning why you even started in real estate...

worried you've made a horrible mistake...

you're stuck and frozen in place...

thinking about going back to your old job...

looking for an excuse to bail out...

can't see yourself as a real estate agent...

Congratulations. You're experiencing a Crisis of Meaning.

A Crisis of Meaning and the entrepreneur's journey

A Crisis of Meaning is one of four phases in the entrepreneur's journey.

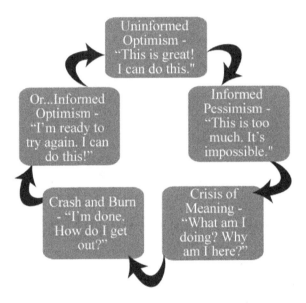

Figure 1 Four Phases of a Crisis of Meaning

Here are the four phases and what they sound like in your head:

- Uninformed Optimism - "This is great! I can do this."
- Informed Pessimism - "This is too much. It's impossible."
- Crisis of Meaning - "What am I doing? Why am I here?"
- Crash and Burn - "I'm done. How do I get out?"
- OR, Informed Optimism - "I'm ready to try again. I can do this!"

Top Agents know all about these phases, and what to do about them.

They know it's an emotional roller-coaster, filled with delight and hysteria, interrupted by moments of chaos and horror.

It's a cycle of phases you'll experience often during your career, but it gets easier as you gain experience.

A Crisis of Meaning is your brain telling you something is unclear.

Your progress grinds to a halt. You've lost focus, purpose, and motivation to move forward.

Your priorities are confused, and you feel lost.

Without clarity, you freeze in place because you don't know what to do next. It's like walking into a dark room in an unfamiliar building. You can't move forward because you can't see. You're afraid.

Most New Agents quit during a Crisis of Meaning because they didn't see this phase coming, nor do they understand why it is happening.

The purpose of a Crisis of Meaning

Every hero's journey passes through moments of testing. True growth cannot happen without it.

It breaks you, and re-shapes you into someone more than you are now.

A Crisis of Meaning is a defining moment in your life.

You will either move forward with a renewed sense of purpose, clarity and determination, or you will regress and eventually quit.

It's a painful moment in your life and career, but among the rare few that are actually worth it.

I can say for certain you will see fruit from this in ways you will never expect.

For now, trust the process and work through your Crisis of Meaning.

Fortunately, Top Agents have shown us that it is possible to overcome a Crisis of Meaning.

And when you make it to the other side, you'll be met with honor and respect from people who have walked the same road before you.

How to overcome your Crisis of Meaning

To conquer the Crisis of Meaning, Top Agents clarify the "WHY" of their lives:

- WHY they do what they do
- WHY they make the sacrifices they make
- WHY they believe what they believe

This is how Top Agents handle failure and success.

Many Top Agents take regular time for introspection.

Self-reflection is a skill they practice every day. Through self-reflection, they strip away the mental clutter so they can focus on what is most important to them.

Self-reflection is like cleaning the mirror.

Keep it clean if you want an accurate picture of your life and your future.

On the other hand, most New Agents don't take the time for self-reflection. Very early in their careers they lose confidence, and then they lose sight of why they became an agent.

Answering your WHY solves your Crisis of Meaning.

When you have a clear answer to your WHY, you gain confidence in every action you take.

Decisions are easier to make. You take action with confidence. Your focus and energy are back, and you're not second guessing.

Clarify the WHY for yourself, and you won't be tempted to quit during your Crisis of Meaning.

"People don't buy WHAT you do. They buy WHY you do it."

~ Simon Sinek

Let's discuss WHY your beliefs are important.

They have a huge impact on your marketing.

If you don't know WHY you believe you're a real estate agent, why would your potential clients believe in you?

Most New Agents can describe WHAT they do, but they can't always articulate WHY they do it.

Simply telling people *what* you do doesn't inspire people to call you. A hundred other agents are also *"what"* they do to everyone in the world.

Others will tell the world *how* they are better than other agents. The problem is it doesn't promise repeat business, because there will always be a "better" agent than you. In essence, you've just pitted yourself against a thousand other agents who out-gun you.

If you want to stand out in the market place, share WHY you are a real estate agent, and WHO you *believe* a real estate agent is to your clients. A person who has clear convictions and solid ethics inspires trust and commitment – especially when those beliefs are shared.

Invest your efforts on sharing your beliefs, and you'll win clients for life. The most powerful bond between two people are the beliefs they share.

Discover your WHY with four questions

When you're in a Crisis of Meaning, discovering your WHY may not be easy.

It's hard to know where to begin, but it's easier than you think.

"The question is the answer." ~ Socrates

Asking the right questions is the best way to end the Crisis of Meaning.

Questions trigger our brains to seek answers.

We are wired as natural problem solvers. The quality of your questions determines the quality of your answers. The right questions will clarify your reasons and life's purpose.

Four questions every client asks you – but won't say out loud

To solve your Crisis of Meaning using good questions, imagine a prospective client interviewing you.

Clients have four questions they silently or verbally ask until they are convinced you are trustworthy. Beware, because they will ask the same four questions a thousand different ways.

1. How did you decide to become a real estate agent? (Origin)

2. What does being a real estate agent mean to you? (Meaning)

3. Why should I trust you? (Morality)

4. What do you hope to accomplish in your career? (Destiny)

It's important to answer these questions for yourself before they surface.

Let's look at the real question behind each question:

1. How did you decide to become a real estate agent?

We all like to know how things began. Clients are no different. They want know your history. Your history defines you and your experiences prove you. Are you from a family of real estate agents? How did you begin? What brought you to this point in your career? What's your story?

2. What does being a real estate agent mean to you?

Answering this question for yourself forces you to clarify your personal beliefs and convictions.

WHY are you an agent? What makes you different? What's your purpose for being a real estate agent?

This very important question defines your life's greater purpose.

3. Why should I trust you?

Clients won't always ask you this directly, but it is always on their minds. This is about your ethics, and what you believe is right from wrong. Ultimately, it defines how you treat your clients, how you will run your business, and the policies you set for yourself and your team. Answering this clarifies your standards and ethics, and inspires your trustworthiness.

4. What do you hope to accomplish in your career?

This is about the future of your relationship with your clients. Will you be there for them tomorrow? Some clients like the idea you are up and coming talent with a bright future. They like to think that they 'discovered' a diamond in the rough, they want a person of lasting value. Without saying it, they want to count on you to be there long after the sale is done.

These are all questions you yourself would ask anyone you're going into business with.

Your answers to these four questions ultimately define you and determine your destiny as a real estate agent.

You don't need perfect answers to each of these questions.

You need only enough to resolve your Crisis of Meaning.

Perfect answers will come in time, as you regularly revisit these questions.

With a clear WHY, you'll lift yourself out of the Crisis of Meaning, and transform into the next stage of the Inner Game: Informed Optimism.

With Informed Optimism, you begin to take action again. You face tomorrow with clarity and purpose and move forward in your business again.

You face the challenges with a clear mind, a smarter strategy, and stronger beliefs.

At each step, you build your confidence.

With a clear WHY and clear beliefs, you win the Inner Game of an Entrepreneur. Because what you believe is the most powerful thing about you.

WHO are you?

All her life, Amy struggled with her weight.

As a young girl, she was always teased at school and was always avoided by the cool kids and never invited to parties. She was never asked to dance, and she was always the last one picked to be on the team.

Early on, she was labeled as a "fat ugly loser."

Today, Amy is in her late twenties, and she's never been able to keep the weight off, even after hundreds of dollars spent on diet and exercise programs.

She's always on the newest trend, hoping that she'll make a breakthrough.

But it's always the same story.

She does well for the first week.

But into the second week, she starts to miss the cake.

She cheats just once. In a matter of days, she falls right back into her old habits.

She can't stop eating the cake!

Amy had a hard time resisting food because food always made her feel better about herself.

But afterwards, she would always sink back into feeling fat, miserable and frustrated.

She felt completely out of control and helpless. Sadly, she eventually believed that there was no hope for "fat ugly losers" like her. She believed she should just accept it and live with it.

After a lifetime of hearing hurtful names, she came to believe she was, in fact, a fat ugly loser. She came to accept the awful names people would call her, and started to repeat it to herself.

In a moment of deep despair, she admitted she hated herself. Amy's negative self-talk filled her mind with Head Trash and lies. She repeated her Head Trash long enough until the lies felt true.

When Head Trash starts to feel true, it becomes a Toxic belief:

- "I failed" turns into "I am a failure."
- "I don't know" turns into "I am stupid."
- "I have been rejected" turns into "I am worthless."

Toxic beliefs ultimately distort your identity and destroy your confidence.

Identity shift from failure to freedom

Rob Scott is a life coach who helped Amy overcome her lifetime struggle with weight.

He specializes in helping people make lasting changes for the better in their lives.

Rob explains that a fundamental shift in a person's core identity liberates them from their toxic and limiting beliefs.

Rob's work with Amy began by changing her self-talk from "I am a fat ugly loser" to "I am an athlete."

She thought it was silly at first. But eventually, her positive self-talk overcame the lies she was telling herself. She behaved more like an athlete and less like a fat, ugly loser.

As she began to believe in herself as an athlete, she started to see results.

She enjoyed exercising and working out, and eating healthier foods. Although she hasn't achieved her ideal weight yet, she has inspired many people at the gym and even her family to live a healthy lifestyle from the changes they saw in her.

She completely committed to herself to a new identity.

Amy has made some lasting changes in her life no diet or pill could offer her.

In less than six months, Amy reversed years of negative, degrading self-talk that had kept her in misery and bondage.

And yes, she still eats cake. But now, it's not a big deal because she knows her limits, and she'll knock out the calories at her next work out.

Because that's what athletes do.

Because she's not a fat, ugly loser. She is an athlete... and cake has no power over her anymore.

What changed?

It was her **core identity**.

Rob removed Amy's Head Trash and toxic beliefs and replaced them with positive and empowering beliefs. It transformed her from a "fat, ugly loser" to a confident, liberated, and healthy woman.

Your core identity defines who you are and what you do.

You become what you believe you are.

Head Trash distorts your beliefs, and disfigures your identity.

A broken identity leads to unhealthy, destructive behaviors.

But healthy, balanced beliefs rooted in truth result in a healthy, liberated life.

What you believe is the most powerful thing about you

Your words about yourself carry tremendous weight. They shape how you value yourself.

As a New Agent, you can experience the same kind of freedom Amy has experienced.

Shifting your core identity to one of a Top Agent redefines your beliefs and refocuses your efforts. Like Amy, when you have a clear identity, nothing can stop you. A deep belief in your calling allows you to endure the disappointments, frustrations, and the testing of your faith.

When you begin to think and behave like a Top Agent, you're able to identify the lies and half-truths that cripple you. Most importantly, you're able to resolve your Crisis of Meaning faster than other New Agents.

Harness your superpower

Every Top Agent has experienced moments of self-doubt and their own Crisis of Meaning.

They know the trial and testing is necessary for a successful career.

Sadly, most New Agents will never overcome the testing of their beliefs and identity.

The critical mistake New Agents make is failing to face their Crisis of Meaning, or worse – ignoring it completely. Doing so ultimately leads to quitting too soon and losing a huge opportunity to enjoy a fulfilling and meaningful career in real estate.

Thousands of successful agents before you have overcome the challenge of self-doubt. In their moments of personal crisis, they always stopped to clarify their beliefs. Specifically, WHY they are here on earth and WHO they are called to be.

If you're experiencing a Crisis of Meaning, you're in a dangerous stage. So take steps to find the truth in your life and clarify your beliefs NOW. Neglecting to face your time of testing intensifies the temptation to quit too soon.

Forgotten experiences are wasted experiences

To experience a Crisis of Meaning, but not learn from it, is a tragedy. To quit during a Crisis of Meaning is a wasted experience. A Crisis of Meaning is your time to forge defining moments in your life. Every successful agent knows it's a painful but valuable stage in your growth.

Keeping a journal of your progress is the best way to learn from your Crisis of Meaning.

For the same reason a good doctor keeps a medical record of your health, a personal journal is an "emotional checkbook" of your progress. Since a Crisis of Meaning is a murky and confusing stage in your journey, you'll need your journal to sort out truth from error in your life.

The process of "reflect and record" protects you from collecting the Head Trash that develops into toxic beliefs.

It's your opportunity to learn from it and grow stronger – or suffer arrested development and eventually quit.

Start your journal today

You don't have to wait for a Crisis of Meaning to begin a journal. Your experiences at any stage of growth is extremely valuable. Recording them helps you accurately recall events and how you responded to them.

Your quality of life is almost always determined by how you respond. Journaling helps you see where you can correct a bad response and enforce a good response.

Use a journal to pause and write out your answers to the four "interview" questions. It's the fastest way to clarify your WHY and WHO, sort out your beliefs, and move forward with confidence toward a satisfying career full of hope, purpose, and meaning.

Find Your WHY and WHO with this simple exercise

1. Start a journal. Try it for 21 days.

It doesn't have to be expensive or fancy. It's just a place to collect and clarify your thoughts. Avoid using a computer, and limit yourself to pen and paper. The act of handwriting your thoughts slows you down and helps you experience deeper reflection on why you are here and who you are. Answer the four "Interview" questions that address your origin, meaning, morality, and destiny. Go deep, and make it specific to your real estate career. The deeper you go, the better your results.

Here's an example:

How did you start? (Origin)

"For practical reasons, I needed to find a way to feed my kids. I asked my real estate agent friends about their experience, and they encouraged me to pursue the idea."

Why? (Meaning)

"We had to sell our house during a difficult divorce. The agent who helped me really came through when I needed it the most. She was patient, understanding and knowledgeable. She was always fighting for me and protecting my interests. Afterwards, I knew I wanted a career where I could be a tremendous help to people who need it most. I believe my experiences have shaped me to serve people who are going through difficult times in their lives."

Why clients should trust you (Morality)

"I've always believed 'what goes around, comes around.' My life has always been guided by this principle, drilled into me by my parents. I'm in this to make friends for life, and living life by the golden rule is the only way to do it right."

What do you hope to accomplish in your career? (Destiny)

"I've decided that my life's mission is to help people in their time of greatest need. My career goals are to perfect my skills, abilities and gain experience to become a valuable friend. Just like the agent who helped me when I needed it most."

2. Commit no more than 15 minutes each day.

Set a timer, if you must. This is not a race, but rather an exercise to focus your thoughts.

Probe as deep as you can into each of the questions. Focus on just one question for the day. Clarity is what you want the most. Remember that you're entitled to specific answers to WHY you are here and WHO you are.

3. Share it.

Choose another agent you trust or a mentor.

Friends and family are good, but only if they have experience with real estate and understand your journey. A mentor is ideal, because they know how your experience will shape you and your character as an agent.

Top Agents have adopted journaling as part of their success plan. It's a habit practiced by great leaders throughout history, from presidents to scientists, pioneers and educators… just about anyone who is changing the world around them.

Like you.

Top Agent Success Principle:

What you believe is the most powerful thing about you.

Next, let's talk about shaping you into an unstoppable force for good!

Chapter 3

What Would You Do If You Could Not Fail?

In the last chapter we talked a lot about beliefs and identity. Now let's talk about believing in YOU.

How a big, fat lie turned out to be a good thing

Business coach Brian Tracy tells the story about a man who was in serious financial trouble.

The man poured all he had into his business, but it was failing miserably. He lost big sales, he was deeply in debt, and his suppliers and creditors were closing in on him. He struggled with declaring bankruptcy, walking away and letting his business evaporate.

So he decided to go for a walk in the park one evening to think it over.

While he was standing on a small bridge overlooking the water, an older man appeared out of the darkness. Seeing Brian's downcast look, the older man stopped and demanded to know what was the matter.

For some reason, the businessman told him about all his financial problems, how his business was collapsing, and why he was giving up on his hopes and dreams of financial success.

The older man listened intently and said, "I think I can help you." He pulled a checkbook out of his pocket, asked the man his name, and then wrote out a check for him. He pushed it into his hand and said,

---

"Take this money. Meet me here exactly one year from today, and you can pay me back at that time."

Then, the older man turned and disappeared into the darkness.

When the businessman returned to his office, he opened up the check. It was for $500,000 dollars. The signature read, "John D. Rockefeller."

He had just received a check for a half-million dollars from the richest man in the world at that time! The same man who formed the Standard Oil Company and who was well known for giving money away to others.

At first he thought he would cash the check and solve all his financial problems.

But then he decided instead he would put the check in his safe, knowing he could draw upon it at any time. He would use this knowledge to deal more confidently with his suppliers and creditors and to turn his business around.

So with renewed enthusiasm he plunged back into his business. He made deals and negotiated settlements, extended terms of payments and closed several large sales.

Within a few months his business was back on top, out of debt and making money.

One year later, he went back to the bridge in the park with the uncashed check still in his hand.

He could hardly wait to tell the older man what had happened.

At exactly the agreed upon time the man emerged from the darkness once more.

Just as the businessman was about to give him back his check and tell him his exciting story of success and achievement over the previous 12 months, a nurse came running out of the darkness up to the old man and grabbed his arm.

She apologized to the businessman saying, "I'm so glad I caught him. I hope he hasn't been bothering you. He's always escaping from the rest home and going around telling people that he's John D. Rockefeller."

She took the old man's arm and led him away.

The businessman stood alone on the bridge, stunned.

All year long, he'd been wheeling and dealing, buying and selling, building his business with a calm, confident knowledge he had a half-million-dollar check in his safe he could cash at any time.

It suddenly dawned on him he had made his business success based on his beliefs, even though the information was false.

His beliefs transformed his self-confidence into real action.

It completely turned his world around.

I love this story, because a lie can expose the truth

The truth is, the man already had the real resources to turn his business around. The resources did not come from the outside, like a check for a half-million dollars. The check was merely "ghost money."

The real "money" came from within him -- his beliefs and identity. It was the source of all his creativity and confidence that moved him into action. When the truth dawned on him, he was set free.

The "money" is in your head, and it's called *confidence*.

You have all you need to succeed in real estate right between your ears.

We all know confidence when we see it.

And it's always a bit annoying when someone else has a lot of it.

But we don't always know what to do when we lose it.

Imagine having the confidence of Muhammad Ali, Michael Phelps, Tiger Woods, Steve Jobs…

What would your life look like if you knew you could never fail at real estate?

You could tell your brother-in-law, the doctor who works 19-hour shifts every day, that you made more money in two days than he did all week.

You could stick it to your ex-boss, the old slave driver, and tell him you're going to Cancun for the week because you had a good month last month. Again.

You could pick and choose the cars you drive, the house you live in, your neighborhood, and the private schools your kids attend.

You could be the person in your neighborhood who makes everyone wonder how you're able to be home for your kids every day.

Unshakeable confidence liberates you

But instead, you might be feeling like Tony.

Today, Tony didn't even feel like getting out of bed. A whack on the snooze button, and he rolls over for another nine minutes. He feels a lot safer staying in bed and sleeping, so he can avoid all the questions he can't answer.

While other agents seem to be doing fine, he doesn't feel like he can endure another day.

Tony feels like he's sinking in quicksand.

Nothing in school or the real estate exam prepared him to build a real estate business.

Somehow, Tony makes it into the office.

Another attempt to fake it again today. If he can pretend like he's doing something important, it might make him feel better about living off his shrinking savings account.

A look at the calendar doesn't inspire him.

Checking email. Responses to blog posts. Twitter. Maybe he should respond. Later. The rest of his day is filled with meaningless busy work. Instead of calling clients, he's cleaning his desk. Polishing his phone. Doodling logos. Previewing new CRMs. Or choosing a new look for his business cards.

Tony is playing business instead of doing business.

Many New Agents know Tony's story.

Habitual procrastination is usually the first sign of low confidence. It's a form of self-sabotaging behavior caused by confused priorities and fear.

In response, people turn to a new marketing system or a new program, or they follow a new real estate guru and spend hundreds of dollars on all the training materials and seminars.

The excitement and determination fades after a few days.

Life gets busy, throws us a curve ball, or another shiny object grabs our face... while we go on collecting more material we don't have time to read.

Later we blame ourselves for lacking the focus and discipline to follow through.

But it's all back to the same cycle: no action.

No action yields no results.

No results produce more guilt, making you feel even worse than before.

Then you're lost in the cycle with confused priorities and taking inappropriate action because of fear.

The Cycle of Fear, the Cycle of Faith, and Building Your Confidence

When you find yourself over-procrastinating, you are likely caught in a **Cycle of Fear**, and it's silently destroying your confidence.

Joshua Boswell is a highly respected business coach and trainer. He does excellent work helping start-ups sort out confused priorities and fears. After working with them, many of his students regain their confidence and restore their momentum toward a productive and profitable businesses.

Joshua explains that the cycle of fear always begins with a lie, a half-truth, misinformation, or false information. The lie creates confusion, which leads to inaction, or procrastination.

To illustrate, let's say you're vacationing on a camping trip and decide to go hiking. The Park Ranger warns you bears have been spotted on several of the hiking trails. He doesn't expect the bears will be out in broad daylight today. But just to be safe, he equips you with a stick, a whistle, some bear spray, and specific instructions on what to do if you encounter bears.

You feel prepared, so you set out on your hike. But in the back of your mind, you're wary of bears.

As you're hiking along the trail, you hear a loud rustling in the woods ahead of you.

So you freeze.

You were warned there were bears.

But since you don't know what's causing the loud rustling noises, you're not moving until you know for sure. Is it a bear, a dog, or the wind?

You don't know what to do until you know what it is. And you'll stay that way until you see the truth. Even the best information and tools are useless if you can't see what's ahead of you.

Fear starts to well up, as you imagine the worse. Your progress grinds to a halt. You're frozen in a state of confusion.

Confusion always leads to inactivity. Inactivity leads to no results.

Hidden truth and lies repeated long enough will distort the vision of your future and imprison you in a state of perpetual confusion and inactivity.

Ultimately, the confusion and inactivity lead you to failure which feeds the lies and casts you down into the cycle of fear and eroding your confidence.

The Cycle of Faith

Boswell goes on to explain that the cycle of faith always begins with truth.

Truth brings clarity, and clarity fosters confidence.

When you see things as they are, you move forward and take action.

Action produces results which paves the way to success, ultimately building your confidence.

As in the case with your hiking trip, once you know it's a bear or a dog or the wind, you know the appropriate action to take.

Action always precedes results you can measure and evaluate.

Top Agents always measure and evaluate their results and make course corrections along the way.

If something didn't work, they evaluate it, change it, or dump it and try again.

This is how success works.

When you see clearly, you take action.

As you take action, you validate your plans which inspires you to move forward or change course – but you never quit. Your faith and confidence grow, leading you to greater success.

Listen to your emotions

Your emotions are a gauge of your health.

When you're feeling depressed or fearful, your emotions are warning you something needs correction. Depression is usually a sign of hopelessness. It's a sense you're stuck in a bad situation with no hope of change. Fear is telling you to avoid something painful. Depression and fear are the worst combination because you know something painful is in store, but you feel powerless to change it.

How to regain confidence like a Top Agent

Top Agents know the journey to success always swings between the cycle of fear and the cycle of faith.

When you're stuck and frozen, you are almost always in a cycle of fear.

But you know you don't have to be a slave to fear.

You can pause, evaluate where you are, and seek out the truth.

A 15-minute confidence booster

One way to gain clarity and separate the truth from lies is to test them with two different statements side by side.

Try this 15-minute exercise. You'll want a timer, a sheet of blank paper, and a pen or pencil.

For best results, try not to type it out. Write this out using pen and paper. The physical act of writing it out slows you down and makes you think through each statement. It also triggers synapses in parts of your brain for deeper cognitive thinking.

At the top of the paper write out: "I cannot because..."

Then, set your timer for five minutes and finish the sentence with as many statements as you can think of before the clock runs out.

Now, pick at least three statements that bother you the most and test them using a modified version of Byron Katie's method for changing your behavior.

Test each statements with these six basic questions:

1. *Is it true?*

2. *Is it absolutely true?*

3. *How do you react, what happens, when you believe that thought?*

4. *What is the opposite thought?*

5. *How does the opposite thought feel?*

6. *What does the new thought inspire you to do?*

Testing each statement allows you to see things as they truly are.

You can eliminate the thoughts that harm you, and liberate yourself from self-sabotaging behavior.

Embrace empowering beliefs

Now, let's dump your Head Trash and toxic beliefs and install empowering thoughts.

On a new sheet of paper, start a new list, and begin with the statement: "I CAN, BECAUSE..."

Set a timer, and write out as many as you can in five minutes.

Review your list, and choose the statements that move you to take action.

As you begin taking the right action again, you'll regain your confidence and build momentum.

It gets easier the more you practice, and train your mind for success like a Top Agent.

You'll recognize the cycle of fear and the cycle of faith, find the truth in your life, and discover that confidence was inside you all along!

Top Agent Success Principle: Confidence in yourself is crucial.

Therefore, take steps to build your confidence everyday.

Section I Summary

* Most agents fail because of unresolved Head Trash and toxic beliefs. But you can dump Head Trash, reverse toxic beliefs, and embrace empowering beliefs.

* Your beliefs are the most powerful thing about you.

* Confidence is fostered by living in truth and eliminating lies.

In Section II, we'll talk about how you can accelerate your progress like a Top Agent, cut your learning curve in half, and adopt the mindset and habits of successful agents.

Section II

The Secrets of Successful Agents

All successful agents share common traits and habits that established their careers.

How they think about their time, money and relationships drives everything they do.

Chapter 4

The Fastest Path to a Steady Income

In one interview, I asked a real estate agent, "What's the hardest thing to do for a first-year agent?"

Her answer was, "Make a steady income."

I asked, "Are you making a steady income now?"

"No."

"Do you want a steady income?" I was curious.

"Of course." She rolled her eyes like it was a dumb question.

"Do you prospect regularly?"

Confidently, she replied: "I go in spurts. I do it when I can get to it."

She seemed proud of her prospecting accomplishments.

I chuckled.

Maybe you can see her obvious problem.

She wants a steady income, but doesn't consistently practice daily money-making activities like prospecting, booking appointments, negotiating, or closing escrows.

Most New Agents don't make the connection – time is money. As a result, they struggle to use their time effectively. At the end of their day, they often wonder what they've accomplished and why the time evaporated so quickly.

When the bills come streaming in at the end of the month, worry, fear, and guilt set in, because they can't account for all the time that has gone by. They have no commission check to show for it.

"Time is money" becomes very real for a New Agent.

Poor time management is the one of the biggest points of failure for New Agents, but it's also the easiest to fix and recover.

Controlling your calendar begins with changing your mind about time.

And when you change your mind about time, you solve a lot of your money problems.

Employee mindset vs entrepreneur mindset

An employee thinks about time differently from an entrepreneur.

For employees, every hour and every day is metered. But their pay check is the same every month.

For entrepreneurs and Top Agents, time is measured by their income at the end of the month.

The better they spend their time, the more income they make.

As Top Agents become more efficient with their time, they make more money.

Trading time vs converting time

Employees *trade* time for money.

In exchange for their days, nights, and weekends, employees are paid a fixed sum of money.

With the exception of an occasional raise or bonus, their income stays the same each year.

In contrast, entrepreneurs and Top Agents *convert* time into money. Every hour spent on their business is converted into an income.

A well-managed calendar can potentially produce an income that is virtually limitless.

Top Agents think like entrepreneurs.

They understand that employees are paid for their time, but Top Agents are paid for their *value*.

YOU, the entrepreneur

As a New Agent, you may not have thought of yourself as an entrepreneur, but you are. As you're building your business, your time is a priceless resource for revenue generating activities.

Failing to control their time is a big reason why so many New Agents quit too soon.

If time is money, then good time management yields a good income.

Master this skill like a Top Agent, and you'll put your money worries to rest.

Measuring success

I want to pause briefly and make one important note.

Money isn't the only way to gauge success.

The most important measure of success is your quality of life and relationships. We've all heard of the guy who's rich but died miserable and alone. A sad cliché.

But you can use money as a measurement because it's easy to count. By counting money, you can see how your marketing plans worked out, the errors in your judgment, lack of discipline, and where you can improve.

As an entrepreneur, you can use money to measure how effectively you've used your time.

Money is never an end itself. Money is an end to a higher purpose: to live with a better quality of life, to be more generous, or to make other people's lives easier.

My to-do list

When I began as an entrepreneur, I tried to manage my time with employee thinking.

So I did what everyone else did: I kept a to-do list. To begin my week, I spent Sunday evening gathering my to-do list of items. It felt great and I was ready to take it all on.

But by Friday evening, less than a third of the items were done, because of unplanned emergencies.

I was left feeling guilty for failing to follow through.

You may think a to-do list would tame your crazy calendar. But ticking off tasks from a list doesn't consistently produce the results you want.

Traditional thinking would say a to-do-list is practical. Yes, it is practical, but it's not always effective.

Why? Employees count time. Entrepreneurs *leverage* time.

What you do with your time is what really matters, not counting time.

Time-management tools

There are thousands of great personal organizers, CRMs, time-management software, and aids to keep track of your time, appointments, and to-do lists. They work well, if you can stay on top of them.

I've tried dozens of them myself, only to later neglect them because of the time it takes to maintain them. I'd spend most of my time organizing my organizer: re-prioritizing, shifting and deferring blocks of task items to different days.

At first, it felt really productive. But later I realized scrambling items on a calendar does not produce an income. I was *playing* business instead of *doing* business.

If organizers work for you – great! Stay with them. Personal organizers and planners are excellent tools. But remember, they are just tools. They won't shift your fundamental view of time.

For the rest of us, we need a core change in the way we think about our time.

When you change your view of time, you change the way you use it, increase your productivity, and consequently your income.

Entrepreneurs organize their time into mini projects with a definite beginning, end, and purpose.

To get the most out of their days, Top Agents assign specific objectives and deadlines to each project. This helps them finish the tasks that yield the best results for generating income.

Give Top Agents 40 hours, and they will produce three times the income of even the best-paid employee.

If time is money, how much are you worth per hour?

A person who believes they are worth $400 per hour naturally manages their time differently from someone who believes they are worth $40 per hour.

Take a glance at the calendar of a Top Agent and compare it with someone who believes they are worth $40 per hour. Their critical activities are vastly different from each other. And Top Agents also have more time for the things they like to do with people they love.

Imagine yourself as an Agent who is worth $400 an hour.

Stop and think how it would change the way you spend your time and money.

For example, do you change the oil on your own car, or pay someone $20 to do it for you?

It might "cost" you an hour for what Speedy Oil Change can do in 15 minutes.

Or did you lose an hour today fixing the printer, or the copy machine, or your computer?

You could instead invest that hour on money-making activities like prospecting, setting appointments, negotiating, or closing escrows.

Focus on closing escrows this month, and you could simply dump the old printer and computer and buy new ones.

Remember your number-one job today is to bring in the cash – something no one else can do for you but YOU.

No one else cares about your bills, providing for your family, or your future.

It's all up to you.

When you believe you are worth $400 per hour, you'll naturally re-prioritize your daily practices and task lists. You'll clearly see why, where, and how you spend your time. You become the kind of person who is worth $400 per hour.

Maybe you don't feel like you're a $400-per-hour agent yet, but you can always start acting like one. The skills and experience will come in time.

Serving your clients like a $400-per-hour agent delivers immeasurable value. Commit to this, and you won't have to go far to find great clients who will love you for life. You'll soon be the agent of choice and grow into the Top Agent you're destined to be.

It may be hard to imagine right now, but there will be a day in your career when earning $400 per hour will seem small. But when you've grown into the kind of Agent who can negotiate the sale of a million-dollar home, you are priceless because of the tremendous value you bring to the negotiating table.

A simple shift in how you think about your time naturally eliminates the activities that choke your career. You'll discover most things disguised as emergencies weren't so urgent after all. Many often take care of themselves.

You'll also find it frees up time for the people most important to you – like your family.

With consistent practice, you'll also see a difference in your bank account at the end of the month.

How to make each day count like a successful agent does

"Sow a thought, reap an act. Sow an act, reap a habit. Sow a habit, reap a character. Sow a character, reap a destiny." ~ Steven Covey

Having consistently productive and powerful days begins with positive daily rituals.

The morning routine is the most important one, because it sets the tone for your entire day.

Your daily habits are what sets you apart from other agents.

Successful agents and entrepreneurs alike all establish a morning routine. They treat the first hours of their day as their most valuable time, so they plan their morning routine around one block of protected time.

According to Vilfredo Pareto, 80% of your productivity comes from 20% of your time.

In an 8-hour day, 20% is 2.5 hours. That means the first 2.5 hours of your day will be most productive, when your willpower is strongest.

When your willpower is strongest, you are in a proactive mode. You control the pace, the tone, and the tasks of your day. Gaining early victories over your task list carries over into the afternoon and allows you room for interruptions, or small changes to your daily schedule.

But missing this window of time triggers your re-active mode. Instead, your day is spent chasing fire engines and putting out fires.

Because your willpower naturally fades throughout the day, it's almost impossible to recover.

Killing a career killer

Poor time management is lethal to all New Agents.

It's one of the biggest reasons 80% will run out of money and quit before their first year. Many look back on their days and weeks and don't realize the time they have wasted on all the wrong goals and activities. The result is zero income.

As a New Agent, your job is to convert your time into money.

But it's hard to do when life assaults you, and everything looks like an emergency. All the seemingly urgent issues control you, dominate your day, and yank you in every direction. Perhaps you're frustrated by repeated, failed plans. Or maybe you're feeling clueless as to what to do next, and you don't want to waste another day wandering aimlessly about while the bills pile up.

The good news is that it's easy to fix.

Design your life for success

Top Agents adopt new habits to gear them toward success.

They are daily habits driven by one simple goal: to get in front of clients.

Consistent practice inspires focused action that promises results.

Just a few small tweaks to your daily routine can re-direct your efforts toward a successful month.

Here's what to do:

1. Plan.

Plan your day the night before.

Set aside just 15 minutes to choose five tasks intended to put you in front of clients, typically in the areas of prospecting and booking appointments. Begin with the tasks which are most difficult or unpleasant for you to do — like cold prospecting.

2. Dedicate.

Dedicate your first 2.5 your hours each morning to completing your five tasks.

If you're like most of us, you'll have to make arrangements. If you have daily morning commitments like getting the kids ready for school, practice your negotiation skills and find a way to make it work for everyone in your family. Most people are reasonable and understand that small sacrifices are required to build your future career.

3. Protect.

Protect your morning work time from all unnecessary interruptions.

It helps to have a friend who will "screen" your calls. Be careful with social media like Facebook and Twitter, especially if you're using them to reach clients. It can easily trap you into long visits and distracting conversations.

Set a timer and work in 20-minute blocks with 5-minute breaks. Productivity studies show that 17 to 22 minutes is optimal work time, with no more than 3- to 5-minute breaks in between. This arrangement intensifies your willpower and boosts your momentum.

Stop your work after 2.5 hours.

If you don't finish your five tasks within 2.5 hours, review it again in the evening and add it to the next day.

If you complete all five tasks early, then take the extra time as a reward.

Adding this kind of focus to your day builds a daily habit that gears you for success.

15 minutes at night before you sleep, and your first 2.5 hours of the day will put you back in control of your calendar, and sharpen your skills of converting your time into money.

Begin now, and get it done!

If you're working part-time to build your real estate business, it's imperative that you begin now.

Good habits take at least 21 consistent days to fully form. Each day you delay is another day without income, while bills and debt accumulate.

Time is something you will never get back. But it's never too late to make small changes today that promise big payoffs tomorrow.

Top Agents focus their most critical and difficult money-making activities in the first 2.5 hours of their day. Early in their careers, they made it part of their morning routine and protected that time for critical tasks. Over time, they gained more clients and experience, and used the hours to expand their skill set to include negotiation prep and closing escrows.

The simple habit of focused time management allowed them to increase their income with each transaction they closed. With regular practice, they naturally became more efficient, which led to earning more per hour.

That's the benefit of converting time into money. As your skills improve, you require less time to do the same tasks, thereby leveraging your time to make more money.

And it all began with the right, simple daily habits!

"We are what we repeatedly do. Excellence, then, is not an act, but a habit." ~ Arsitotle

Top Agent Success Principle:

Master your calendar, and you will master your money.

Now that we've defined your relationship with time and money, let's build on that and talk about how you can boost your growth and accelerate into becoming a Top Agent.

Chapter 5

Try This Instant Career Booster

At the rise of his career, Tiger Woods was good but not great. He had a dilemma with bunkers (also known as sand traps) sabotaging his golf game. The PGA ranked him number 61 in sand saves.

In school, 61 is barely a passing grade.

Corporate America would have dumped their stocks in Woods, and the PGA wouldn't have given him a second look.

It was a glaring weakness in Tiger's game that would cripple his career.

You would think he would go to work lowering his sand saves, and raise his ranking.

And he did. But not perfectly.

Tiger did something different. He learned perfect sand saves would not win the game. He didn't need a perfect score in sand saves. Instead, Tiger worked on sand traps only enough to get him out the bunker.

You see, the game isn't won by how many sand traps you can dig out of.

It is won by getting the ball closest to the hole.

So Tiger chose to focus his time and effort on perfecting his most dominant strength: his swing.

Particularly his drive.

Tiger's most powerful skill was his ability to drive the ball with howitzer-like force and laser-point accuracy. Perfecting his power and accuracy by placing the ball within inches of the hole would mean he could avoid the bunkers altogether. Sand traps would no longer pose a problem.

Tiger chose to focus on his strength rather than his weakness.

The true test came at the British Open at Saint Andrews where there are more bunkers than any other course. Over a four-day period, Tiger Woods never landed in a bunker. Not once.

He went on to win the British Open at the age of 24 – two years younger than Jack Nicklaus.

Woods held the record for most strokes under par in the Masters, the U.S. Open, and the British Open.

The cost of conventional wisdom

We focus our energies too much on fixing our weaknesses, often at the cost of our own strengths.

Left on his own, Tiger Woods would have followed conventional wisdom. Instead, he embraced a different approach that changed his career forever.

Unconventional wisdom yields uncommon results

Tiger Woods didn't figure out his strategy on his own. He had help. He hired a coach and mentor.

Great mentors rarely dish out conventional wisdom.

Because conventional wisdom gives you average results.

Mentor Butch Harmon transformed Tiger's career. It was Harmon who identified Tiger's strengths and choose to perfect them, rather than expend all his energies on his weakness. Butch knew Tiger didn't need a perfect score in sand saves. He just need to be good enough to consistently dig himself out.

Butch coached Tiger so his weakness didn't undermine his strengths.

Unconventional wisdom gives you uncommon results.

Butch saw in Tiger what Tiger could not see in himself. Only a few small changes to Tiger's swing made a huge difference – a difference big enough to eliminate the threat of bunkers and catapult Tiger's career into an international success.

As a result, Butch Harmon coached Tiger Woods to eight of his 14 major titles.

A great mentor can identify and unlock your potential

A great mentor does more than simply point out your weakness and fix it. A great mentor will show you how to exploit your strengths, so you can live empowered and liberated.

A mentor will help you get unstuck when you're stuck. Guide you out of an ethical mess.

Help you deal with a bad client. Prop you up when you're beat down. Ignite you into taking action. Keep you accountable to your goals. Challenge you to dream big. Accelerate your learning curve so you meet your goals in half the time.

If you want a great career, a mentor can be your real guide to extraordinary success. It's worth every minute of your time to pursue a good mentor.

Talk to any great agent, and they'll give credit to the mentors in their life for their careers.

Success is better caught than taught

We learn best by mimicking. In fact, we're hardwired to imitate.

We've all been doing it since we were infants and all through our childhood.

When I was four years old, I copied everything Superman did with my red boots and make shift cape. I believed I was Superman. Then I sprained my ankle on the landing while trying to fly off the backyard porch. That suspended my career as Superman, but it didn't change my desire to imitate him.

You'd be surprised at how much you start to sound like your mom or dad when you get older.

If you're a mom or dad now, you may have caught yourself talking and acting like your parents with your own kids.

And that happens without us knowing it.

But imagine if was an intentional, conscious effort to emulate leading performers in our field.

Mirroring and shadowing Top Real Estate Agents is the best and fastest way to become a Top Agent. To become a great agent, hang out with great agents.

How to find a good mentor

Locating a good mentor is easy.

Many real estate agents have suggested looking in a non-competing area and attending an open house. You can network there until you find leads to the Top Agents in that area. Or collect contact info on all the best agents in that area from websites and social media.

Once you've identified them, spend a week following their social media posts, websites, and other marketing channels. Watch how they respond and interact with their followers, and decide if you'd like to

E. Theodore Aranda

emulate their style. If they're someone you can follow, then they're a good candidate. A few agents I interviewed note this important consideration because you become like those you follow. You're choosing them as much as they are choosing you.

Be sure you like and respect them and that they model the kind of agent you want to be. *Consider more than their income level.* You'll learn faster and your journey to the top will be much more fulfilling.

How to approach a good mentor

This can be awkward for New Agents.

Before you approach potential mentors, be prepared with something valuable to offer them.

After all, you're planning to ask for their most precious resource – time. So it pays to have a genuine interest in helping them.

Sometimes, they'll tell you exactly what they want in return. Listen and deliver. Offering to help first opens up what could otherwise be an awkward conversation.

Watch and listen very carefully for their specific needs or desires. Be creative and generous here. Go beyond the typical offer of coffee, lunch, or dinner.

One agent offered his mentor pool cleaning services for a year. Another one had weekly groceries sent to his mentor's home after the mentor and his wife had a baby.

My favorite story is how one agent discovered his mentor had an avid interest in 17th century sailing ships. So he found a cruise line that sails restored 17th century ships from Avalon to San Diego. He booked a four-day tour for his mentor, and they've been friends ever since.

Shortly after, he offered to help with office work – something he knew his mentored loathed.

61

The point is, be a person of value before you ask for something of value.

Accelerate your career with three important relationships

The first relationship is your career mentor.

But there are two other mentoring relationships that are just as important and extremely valuable: a mentoree and a peer mentor.

Take on a mentoree

It's often true when you have to teach a subject, you learn more, retain more, and prove your depth of knowledge. Pay It Forward, and share what you've learned! A mentoree benefits from you as much as you benefit from them.

Take on a peer mentor

"Iron sharpens iron, so one person sharpens another." ~ The Proverbs of King Solomon

Professional boxers and semi-professional boxers have a sparring partner. Usually, it's another boxer of the same or slightly better skills and experience. The tremendous value is the accountability and daily practice.

Your peer mentor also shares with you a similar stage in the journey. When things get rough, you'll have a fellow "traveler" who immediately understands you and what you're going through.

Real estate is built on the strength of relationships. Your success depends on it.

Your most important professional relationships will be with your mentor, the people you mentor, and your peer mentor.

Mary's accelerated success

Mary is an extraordinary Top Agent.

As a young single mother, she had to do something to raise her four boys, so she chose to be a real estate agent.

She had to learn fast how to sell houses.

The bills were piling up, and with four mouths to feed, she had precious little time to waste.

The fast track, she recalls, was to listen a lot and shadow and mirror great agents. She sat in the office and quietly observed.

She went to open houses and listened to good agents interact with potential clients. Then she took a risk, put herself out there and approached the best agents to shadow. She sold her first home in a month, and hasn't looked back since.

As her kids were growing up, she never missed a soccer game, football game, or parent meeting.

In fact, one day her son asked her if she was a drug dealer. Shocked, she asked him why.

"Because," he said curiously, "You're always home. No one ever sees you leave for work and you're always driving the nicest cars in the neighborhood."

Mary, like many other successful agents interviewed, credits her rise to success to her mentors. Not to high dollar marketing tools, hours of seminars, or hundreds of dollars spent on training videos of real estate gurus.

Her success strategy was simple: listen, learn, and imitate the best.

Reclaim your dreams

If you're feeling stuck and alone, then you may have fallen into isolation.

It usually happens in the absence of a mentor or support group in your life.

Without a mentoring team (mentoree, peer mentor, and mentor) to drive and guide you, your growth is arrested. You've ceased prospecting for clients or following up on leads, and you're making excuses at the end of your day. Your goals and plans to build your real estate business are neglected until they drown in the undertow of life along with your hopes and dreams.

Most New Agents in this condition won't ask for help. They believe they will sort it out on their own. But they typically never get around to it, and eventually join hundreds of others who quit too soon.

Finding a mentor is easier than you think.

You'd be surprised how supportive Top Agents are to a New Agent. They've been where you are now, and they know submitting to a mentor is the best thing for you.

Get connected and grow

Approaching a mentor is so very critical to your success that it deserves your focused efforts.

1. *Set a deadline date to approach a mentor. Allow yourself no more than 10 days.*

Put it on your calendar and commit to this date. Have at least three names chosen.

2. *Before the deadline date, consider the three people you have chosen.*

Take time to observe how they interact with clients and other agents. If they fit your style, then they are good candidates.

3. *Once you've made your choice, find something of value to offer them.*

They might need help with office work, or a favorite hobby. Learn what they want or need, and be prepared to offer more than a cup of coffee or lunch.

4. *Ask. Be very specific.*

Practice your negotiation skills. Make your offer and ask for an hour of their time, over lunch once a week for three weeks. Be specific about what you'd like to discuss in that lunch hour.

Mention at the end of three weeks, you'll evaluate your time together and decide if you'd both like to continue.

If they decline, don't fret. Offer the option to try again another time, or call the next person on your list.

Most Agents will be happy to help you. When you begin meeting, have your topics prepared and watch the clock carefully. When your hour comes to a close, be the first to remind them and give them the option to stop. Always allow them the choice to go longer if they wish.

Find a mentor now

The longer you are stuck and isolated, the more likely you are to quit. Eighty per cent of this year's New Agents will discover this to be true. It takes very little effort to allow your real estate career to die a quiet death.

Only 20% of the New Agents this year will make it their first priority to find a mentor. It's a safe prediction that they will flourish and grow by this time next year.

Delaying your search for a mentor is costly. Considering the time you've spent spinning your wheels, overwhelmed, confused, and frustrated, you're probably feeling like you're not where you'd like to be in life right now.

A mentor is your best way to make up for lost time, accelerate your progress, and get the support you need to get going and keep going.

And, it's the only way to get long-lasting results.

So set a deadline date to begin the process of finding a mentor now.

It's time to re-ignite your dreams back to life!

Top Agent Success Principle: A mentor, a peer mentor, and a mentoree are your three most valuable friends as you grow into a Top Agent.

Treat them like gold.

In the next chapter, discover the one thing that defines you as the agent of choice.

Chapter 6

The Benefit of Doing the Right Thing Even
When It Hurts

During my interviews with real estate agents, I've often heard it said real estate agents rank somewhere in between used car salesmen and lawyers.

It's true many consumers feel that way. Many have been betrayed and exploited and played for a fool.

To compare, buying a car is high stakes and feels a lot like buying a house. Lots of money and emotion are stirred. Both involve mounds of paperwork. Both transactions make a perfect cocktail of joy, anger, elation, disgust, fulfillment and rage. And the process is as fun as three hours in a dentist's chair – sans Novocain.

I've seen, or been a victim to, a lot of car buying scams: bait and switch, the "low monthly payments" deal, low-balling the trade-in, title washing, misleading pricing, odometer fraud, stealing the deposit.

If you've ever been milked by a devious sales person, you'll recall very quickly why you dislike salespeople. The damage stays with us for longer than we care to remember, while we live with the embarrassment and shame of being played for a fool.

You never forget or forgive a salesman who exploited you.

I blamed the salesmen. But in the end, I had to blame myself.

Perhaps that's why it's so uncomfortable when the tables are turned, and *you're* the sales person.

Ever notice when you cold call, your heart is pounding, your hands tremble, sweat forms on your brow, and the phone feels like a boat anchor?

It's likely because you fear the judgment of being labeled as a crooked salesman. It's unfair, to be sure. You're an honest person, just trying to feed your kids.

It's truly unfair for all the genuinely honest and hardworking car salesmen, real estate agents, and lawyers who live by high personal standards.

Don't cross that line!

Most real estate agents don't begin their days planning to exploit their clients.

But the season of testing always rises when you haven't landed a client in weeks, haven't closed a sale in months, your marketing budget has spun out of control, and the creditors are sending you nasty letters.

And now, you're willing to tell a little white lie just to close escrow.

One small act of betrayal begins a habit of compromise. Over time, bad habits forge character traits unbecoming of a Top Agent.

Five things bad real estate agents teach us about ethics

You'd be surprised at the number of "seasoned" agents who can't tell the difference between right and wrong. Over time, they thoughtlessly practiced what was "acceptable" without questioning it.

If you're ever unsure, simply recall the times in your life when you were exploited by a crooked salesman.

Always live by Golden Rule of "treat others as you would treat yourself."

Putting yourself in your client's shoes will clear the ethical fog in a hurry.

Here are five examples of questionable ethics. These aren't illegal, but they are shady.

1. Showing preference for your own listings or your company's listings

Hiding listings from your client is questionable, especially if it affects your commissions.

As the Buyer's Agent, show ALL the listings. You might get grief for doing so, because your office will make you feel like you're going against the team. But hiding listings is still shady because it brings into question your fiduciary trust.

2. Hiding for-sale-by-owner homes from your client

If you honestly didn't know about a FSBO, then you're off the hook. But if one pops up in your search, you're bound by duty to show it. This is an ethics question because it's easy to play blind to it. The real question is, what will you do when no one is looking?

3. Hiding referral fees

If you ever have to refer your client to another agent, your client deserves to know your referral fees. It proves you are confident about the referral, and you aren't shuffling your client away to an unknown wolf. Furthermore, it demonstrates you know the quality of service and value the other agent offers. Be transparent.

4. Delivering poor service because of low commissions

This one's on you, if you decided to take on the client. If the commission was just too low, then you should have passed on it. But if you took it on anyway, don't compromise on your quality. Take it as a learning lesson and choose differently next time. When you compromise, you put your reputation and your name at risk. Lose your good name, and you've lost everything.

Instead, you have an opportunity to deliver outstanding value and collect great referrals.

Again, this is a question of ethics because it's not clearly wrong or illegal. But compromising your quality of service is a bad habit that will erode your reputation over the course of your career.

5. Taking on a less-than-perfect listing

You know it won't sell. But you know you can prospect for new clients during the marketing campaign. You have a ripe opportunity to pick up unrepresented buyers. Some agents charge additional marketing fees, staging fees, and miscellaneous fees to cover their marketing costs.

All the while, they're feeding false hopes to their seller on the seller's dime.

It's not illegal, but it's not ethical either to offer an unrealistic promise to the seller. This is set up to your advantage, not your client's.

If you ever wonder if your client should know the truth, fault on the side of transparency. Even if it hurts. Your clients deserve to know the truth about how the market will respond to their property.

They are relying on your honest expert opinion.

Additionally, they should know you're prospecting for new clients as well as selling. If it's acceptable to the client and it doesn't interfere with the clients' desires, then you're free to pursue it.

In the end, good ethics protects your relationships and builds your integrity. When things get desperate, resist the temptation to compromise your ethics. Also beware of clients who will test you.

Remember that compromising your ethics offers short-term gain for long-term pain.

This isn't intended to be an exhaustive lesson on good ethics, but it's a start on cultivating good habits like Top Agents.

One important point to remember:

What is ethical is always legal. But what is legal is not always ethical.

What goes around comes around

Many Top Agents have lived by this phrase, and they all say it has served them well.

This is all about the stuff – both good and bad – that floats to the surface later in your career.

You never know when and where, but it always comes back to haunt you or bless you.

Cultivating good ethical habits protects you from short term gain and long term pain. In the bigger picture, your ethics determines how far you go in this industry. We want you to enjoy all the success you deserve.

What your clients want from you, but will never say to your face

Most of the time, they don't know how to say it or ask for it. Much of it is because they won't ask for it from someone they don't yet trust.

It's clouded by a narrative in their minds painting an unflattering picture of you.

It's the picture of a used car salesman with your face pasted on.

Applying good ethics here will quickly repaint their picture of you and earn the trust of your client by giving them what they want before they ask.

Here's a basic psychology of what goes on in your client's head.

Give your clients these five things before they ask, and you'll quickly and ethically build trust with your clients.

1. Give me choices.

"I like choices because it makes me feel like I am in control.

"Choices empower me and make me feel better about my decision to buy a house from you. I'm putting a lot at risk and I'm terrified of what I might lose. Give me choices and information so I can feel confident in making decisions. I want an advisor and a coach. Not a salesman."

2. Build up my confidence.

"If you build up my confidence and tell me I can do this, my trust in you will soar. I feel threatened because you're the expert and I am not. Do not ever patronize me. That will cost you your contract with me, and with any of my family or friends.

When it sounds like I am telling you how to do your job, it's because I've lost confidence in myself, not you. Stay ahead of me, lead me, and have answers to my questions before I ask. Make me believe you believe in my plans."

3. Assure me.

"When things start to feel uncertain, I am going to become defensive. That's when I look to you the most, and it's how I will evaluate you as an agent. I want assurances you are always fighting for my best interests. Do this, and I will love you for life.

"If I reward you with the listing contract, what's your plan to sell my home? Can I trust you to lead me through this process? What's your plan? What will it cost me? Will you be transparent with me even if it's bad news? If the deal starts to go sideways, can I rely on you to fix it? Are you willing to share the risk with me?"

4. Make me feel like we're on the same team.

"I hate feeling left out of the loop on anything regarding this deal. I never want to be the last to know to anything. I hate it most when I feel naïve, and I fear the embarrassment of being played for a fool. From the beginning, treat me more like a business partner rather than a client. That makes me feel like we're on the same team working toward the same goals."

5. I want what's fair.

"I want what's fair. I don't consider myself greedy, but the minute I perceive an imbalance, I become cynical and question your honesty. I want complete clarity on what is equitable. Don't confuse me. Make everything easy for me to understand, and I'll stop scrutinizing your character."

New Agents miss these subtle signs completely. Top Agents know them intuitively.

Other agents have ignored them and have even carried it through to a successful sale – but sadly, at the sacrifice of their client's experience.

Those agents probably didn't last very long, and probably they weren't aspiring to be Top Agents.

With the competition so fierce, you can be extraordinary by giving your clients these five things before they even ask. It practically assures you of your next deal or leads you to your next client.

Remember that this is all about building trust through good ethics. It's about the long game, and it's how all the Top Agents play it.

Stay a step ahead of your clients

Now that you know what your clients are really thinking, you can dismantle their natural resistance.

Give your clients confidence and assurance and treat them equitably, and they will reward you with their loyalty.

Prove your value with good ethical practice, and they will never question your commission or your advice.

Building a reputation of solid ethics earns you the respect and right to be heard anywhere.

And that, by far, is the best compliment you could ever earn that offers true lasting value.

It's the material that all Top Agents are made of.

Even inexperienced agents find success when they conduct themselves with high ethical standards. Honesty and integrity always wins over incompetency.

Commit to embracing and practicing good ethics, and you'll never have to pay for leads or look for work ever again.

We are defined by what we know, verified by what we do, and judged by how we treat people.

Top Agent Success Principle: Live by the Gold Rule.

What is legal is not always ethical; What is ethical is always legal.

In the next chapter, learn a controversial method of achieving success. Paying it forward is all about giving back, and it can instantly elevate you to the next level.

Chapter 7

Give and Grow Rich

This is from a book called, *The Fall of Fortresses* by Elmer Bendiner. Elmer Bendiner was a flight navigator in a B-17 during WW II.

During a bombing run over Kassel, Germany his B-17 was showered by flak from Nazi anti-aircraft guns. That was not unusual, but this time, their fuel tanks took direct hits.

The 20 millimeter shells piercing the fuel tanks would have surely set off an explosion, but no such thing happened. They landed back at base safely with most of the bomber and crew intact.

The morning following the raid, Bohn Fawkes, the pilot, visited the crew chief to ask for the magical shell that pierced their tanks without an explosion. He wanted the shell as a souvenir of unbelievable luck.

The crew chief told Bohn that not just one shell -- but 11 shells had been found in the gas tanks.

Eleven unexploded shells!

Just one live shell would have blasted the mighty B-17 out of the sky and ended the lives of the all its crewmen aboard.

"It was as if the sea had been parted for us. A near-miracle, I thought."

Bohn explained the shells had been sent to the armorers to be defused.

Apparently, when the armorers opened each of those shells, they found no explosive charge.

"They were clean as a whistle and just as harmless."

But not all of them were empty. One contained a carefully rolled piece of paper.

On it was a message scrawled out in Czech. Upon translating the note, we were stunned and marveled at its message. The note read:

"This is all we can do for you now... Using Jewish slave labor is never a good idea."

Opportunities to change the world surround us all day, every day. One act of kindness can change the course of history at any moment.

Those Jewish laborers fought the war in their own way, in the best way they could.

But the real lesson here is that every effort, however small, makes a huge difference to someone else.

A small act of kindness resulted in saving the lives of those airmen that day.

But as those airmen later went home after the war, it also had a lifelong impact on their families and children, and eventually their grandchildren. Generations of people were spared from the ravages of war.

All from one simple and thoughtful act of kindness.

You can't put a price tag on what changes history.

Paying it forward is a premeditated act of kindness

When you take action to solve a specific problem by donating your time and/or money, you're paying it forward.

The key is preemptive acts of kindness that bless, surprise and delight. They are planned and measured responses to meet a known need.

Many Top Agents regularly practice paying it forward. They are known in their communities as more than "just" real estate professionals. Over time, they built solid relationships with the families and businesses in each of their neighborhoods.

All from paying it forward.

The way it works is beautiful in its simplicity

If you've ever been the recipient of an act of kindness, you know how it changes you.

It triggers something inside you to give back.

And it doesn't stop there. It's contagious. One small act of kindness can spark a movement.

This kind of thinking is rare among many New Agents because it doesn't have an apparent or tangible payoff.

But Top Agents know that it can pay *tenfold*.

Paying it forward makes you a better agent

It changes the way people view you in the communities you serve. When they see the value you bring to their neighborhood, people are more likely to trust you.

And when they trust you, they are inspired to adopt you as their Agent of Choice.

At a rudimentary level, paying it forward is far more cost effective than printing and pasting flyers all over the neighborhood. At this point in your career, you want to do things inexpensively and effectively with near instant results.

Acts of kindness achieve that.

At a higher and more profound level, adopting a habit of paying it forward allows you to leave a legacy of kindness that is long remembered after you're gone.

It promises you a long-lasting, fulfilling, and rewarding career on every level: relationships, achievement, impact, income, legacy.

Your real estate business can be an instrument of good works in your community

By adopting a policy of paying it forward, you can set good habits to build a strong community and a loyal client base.

There are a thousand different ways to pay it forward in your business.

The best way to begin is by walking the neighborhoods you serve and then watch, look and listen. You'll see opportunities to do good all around you.

It can be as simple as serving in an inner city soup kitchen for an hour, or delivering a box of groceries to a single mother of three, simple yard work for an elderly widower, organizing a community picnic, or participating in a Saturday morning mini marathon.

Practice paying it forward consistently, and watch how your personal life changes – and how your business changes.

Then watch the neighborhood transform itself into a place where everyone wants to live.

"Only the life lived for others is worth living." ~ Albert Einstein

Top Agents pay it forward

Top Agents choose to live a pay-it-forward life.

They make generosity part of their daily habits until it eventually became part of who they are.

And it flows naturally from their business.

It goes beyond wishing someone a nice day.

Top Agents became experts at spotting opportunities to bring the right solutions at the right time at every situation. That mindset allowed them to be exceptional agents.

They know good will always earns you the right to be heard. Being heard is always the first sign of trust any stranger will grant you, and usually it's the beginning of great friendships.

You may feel like you're too broke to pay it forward, but this is not about money. Being broke is a temporary condition, but being poor is a chronic state of mind. Paying it forward is about preparing yourself for true wealth through character and integrity.

The benefit behind a pay-it-forward life is to live free from the power of money. Our natural tendency is to own and control the things we have. Greed weaves itself into our hearts, and before we know it, money and possessions take control of our lives.

But the wise Agent knows that in the end, you can't take any of it with you.

A wealthy mindset is cultivated through the habits of kindness and generosity. You always have something to offer in the form of time or money or both. Giving is the most powerful thing you can do to make a difference in your lifetime.

An amazing life begins by paying it forward.

Paying it forward is about leaving the world a better place than how you found it

Remember this core rule of paying it forward: It is a premeditated act of kindness expecting nothing in return.

It doesn't matter where you are, or what you have, you always have something you can give away to make someone else's life better.

If you're ready to create something amazing in your life, begin by paying it forward today.

You just might be the miracle that someone needs right now.

Top Agent Success Principle: One act of kindness can change history.

You're on the right path now! Don't stop.

Next, learn about finding your specialty and choosing your niche for maximum effectiveness.

Chapter 8

What The Real Estate Exam Didn't Teach You About Prospecting

You know you have to do it. Your broker knows you have to do it. So to get it over with, he tosses you a phone book and tells you to start making calls.

Beads of sweat form on your forehead. Your face feels like it's on fire. Your hands tremble as you pick up and dial the phone. It feels like a cold, 800-pound boat anchor against your head.

As the dial tones pulse in your ear, you're secretly hoping they won't pick up. You give yourself a quick a pep talk: "Follow your script. Try not to sound like an idiot robot."

More dial tone, as your stomach is twisting into a knot.

One last ring tone, and voice mail kicks in.

Relief. Now you can hang up and try again later. ...Maybe.

Deep breath. Next number. Reset, then start over. Again.

While you're chipping away on that, your broker drops on your desk another long list of old leads and a county map.

"Pick a farm," he grunts, pointing to the map.

Now the real fun begins.

Farming neighborhoods is a lot like sailing out into open sea in hopes of catching fish. You must rely on your best guess.

With a little luck, you cast your best "bait" in spite of the hundreds of fishermen who have canvassed these waters before you.

This method of generating leads is where many new agents start – and end – their careers.

After you stake your territory to farm, there follows all the activity intended to tell the world you're a real estate agent.

You write your best elevator pitch and cram it onto business cards, postcards, refrigerator magnets, signposts, tee shirts, hats, banners, notepads, flyers, brochures... all plastered with your name, face, phone number, and email.

Then you work the farm every day, plaster the neighborhood with flyers, send out postcards every two weeks, and hope someone – anyone – calls you.

Oh, and by the way, you're paying for all the printing and media costs *every month...*

And we haven't even covered social media, Zillow, or Redfin yet.

It gets real expensive real fast.

To keep you in the game (until your money runs out), everyone tells you that "you gotta spend money to make money..."

What if you found out that prospecting this way is backwards?

It's backwards because it's like fishing for anything that bites.

You're *guessing* where the hungry fish are, and *guessing* what bait to use.

Guessing is the worse way to fish. It's costly and a waste of time.

But... if you're fishing for trout, you'll go to the streams where trout live and use bait you know trout will like.

That one difference makes you smarter than 80% of the "fishermen" out there.

Top Agents know; amateurs guess

Most New Agents were trained to market their business by guessing.

When you "farm a neighborhood," you make your best guess by casting anything out there in hopes anyone with a pulse will respond.

There is nothing wrong with farming neighborhoods. It's just not the best place to start for a New Agent, because it's costly and the results are often dismal.

Although it does have the potential to generate leads, farming is unsustainable for a hopeful New Agent with a shoestring budget.

When it fails, you can't help feeling you're to blame, because it relies on you to make it work.

Everyone tells you you're not working hard enough. But working harder isn't going to cram your calendar with eager prospects dying to talk to you.

It's not your fault. You were just doing what you were told.

It's a faulty system with a faulty premise, and it's become a lazy way to train a New Agent.

It's time to work smarter.

There's a much easier way that takes much less time and money.

Specialize in a specific market

Narrow your focus to a first time buyer, military, divorced, condos, single family homes, rentals. Choose one group of people or dwelling type.

Then create a profile of your ideal client.

A friend of mine who is a financial advisor has clients who are real estate agents. They market specifically to pet owners who are age 50 and older. They spend over $150,000 per year in marketing.

That's a crazy budget for a *very* narrow niche.

But they'd *have* to spend that much just to find clients, right?

Their best year?

They broke one million dollars in sales in 2014.

That's 15% of their income spent on marketing to the *right* people.

This year, they are on track to earn at least $850K (only because the market has slowed a bit).

Still, a lot of New Agents can live on just 10% of that.

Specialists are paid higher than generalists. On average, about 32% more across the board, in industries other than real estate: financial advisors, counseling, consulting, marketing, any client/service-based industry. It's also true in other industries like healthcare and manufacturing.

Specializing and serving a specific market is simply more cost effective.

Specialists run a leaner business because they spend less on marketing and personal resources to reaching just a select few, not the entire population.

As a specialist, it's easier to find clients who love you, and decline clients who don't appreciate you.

It's even easier to build rapport with them because you can speak to their specific needs. And by specializing, you eliminate most of the competition.

Narrowing the field makes your job 80 times easier. Instantly.

It may seem counter-intuitive, but it really makes business sense.

For example, let's say you decide to specialize in estate sales. Where would you find qualified leads? The easiest sources would be the obituary columns of the local newspaper. Check the probate records at city hall. Go hang out with financial planners, and real estate lawyers at your local REIA. These professionals will always need the services of an agent for their clients, and sometimes for themselves. You're helping them by taking care of their clients.

Building relationships with these professionals will expand your leads and lead sources dramatically – for the least amount of work and cash.

As a specialist in estate sales, you'll be the hero who brings relief and resolve for a family who needs peace the most.

Another example is land development. Where would you find qualified leads?

Check with local architectural and engineering firms and ask about their latest projects.

As you drive about town, look at construction sites. They will usually have the contracting company posted with a website or contact info. Each work site is an opportunity for them to advertise their services.

Taking note of their web address, and spending 5 minutes on Google will get you all the information you need to start digging deeper for qualified leads.

Check the land developer companies, and see where they are building and planning. Check the Land Development Offices at City Hall. Look for the areas where they are planning to build new power, water and sewer lines. That's a huge clue.

The golden list is the one with developers and contractors bidding to buy the land. That alone will give you an instant edge on the competition. Find out what they're building, then move in early and position yourself as the "go to" agent.

As a specialist, your chances of being the agent of choice are greater against other agents who are generalists. You'll build rapport faster because you can swiftly speak to their needs. And you'll spend less time justifying your commission fees – perhaps even raising them – because most clients expect a specialist to be more valuable.

In the time it takes you to farm a neighborhood, you can find the right contacts who will yield a much greater chance of turning into qualified leads.

Tips on choosing a specialty

Start with who you know from past work experience, or even your hobbies. Those people all need a home, and they will all need a real estate agent like you.

Or pick your favorite relatives and ask them what they do for a living. If you like what they do, invite them to lunch and meet them at their offices where you can talk to their friends. It's a lot easier than cold calling.

You can always start in your "sphere" for practice but plan to expand very quickly, because your friends and family may not trust you as a serious real estate agent.

You can approach this by industry. Check out the Standard Rate and Data Service. It's a directory listing of active businesses and media lists for direct mail, online readers for consumer magazines, newspapers, radio, and TV.

You can access lists to specifically targeted audiences. It's not free, but you can access it through the library with a valid library card. It's a handy marketing tool, but for your purposes, it's a place to target specific industries for potential leads.

The SBA (Small Business Administration) is a place to browse government-oriented industries, mainly civilian government contractors who sell their goods and services to government agencies. You can search by state or by industry by NAICS (*North American Industry Classification System*) code or DUNS (*Data Universal Number System*) numbers.

You are looking for the market size, particularly the number of paid subscribers. Paying customers validates the size and interests of a market. Reading what they read will show you their interests and give you plenty to talk about when you begin contacting them.

Become an expert and never pay for leads again; have new clients calling YOU

You have your list of leads. Now what?

Don't send out flyers just yet.

First, do a bit of research by asking some questions. You want to find out what your specific audience desires and what keeps them awake at night.

For example, young military families are prone to frequent relocation. It has a huge impact on their kids. So, become an expert at finding excellent schools in the area or neighborhoods with lots of kids and welcoming communities. Find environments that will help their kids make friends.

Find out what your niche wants, and what's keeping them from getting it.

Look beyond the obvious. The deeper you look, the better.

Find their point of pain and offer solutions.

Address their needs before they ask, and you'll build instant rapport and credibility, and you'll demonstrate your incredible value.

Presto! You've just established yourself as an expert. They'll love you forever.

You can learn how to do this in one weekend, and it won't cost you a cent.

Once you have your targeted list, then you can plan your marketing efforts. But this time, you'll know exactly what to say on your postcards and flyers to speak to relevant topics, information and points of conversation to your audience.

Now you're operating with knowledge like a pro, not guessing like an amateur.

Dedicate at least two hours each day to reach your audience. Protect that time, and make it a consistent activity. It is the most valuable two hours you have every day to build a healthy and growing real estate business, and the life you're creating.

If you haven't read it yet, check out Chapter 4, which talks about time management and getting the most out of your day.

Top Agent Success Principle: Stop guessing.

Lower your risk by specializing and knowing your market.

Read on to learn the one skill that makes you the most highly valued agent

Chapter 9

Learn This Skill to Bring in the Cash

Every agent has the same access to the all same marketing data, and the same opportunities.

But what separates a good agent from a great agent – and great agents from Top Agents – is the skill of negotiation.

Master this skill, and you'll never be out of work.

Negotiating your commission is a huge issue, and you can learn to do it well.

What to do when clients don't want to pay your commission

As a New Agent, one of the most uncomfortable conversations you'll have with a client is over your commission. Clients love to "negotiate" your commission fees (talk you down).

Don't be surprised. Just like you and me, everyone wants to feel like they're getting a good deal. That means you'll have to justify your value.

It's tempting for a New Agent to lower their fees. After all, you think it's an opportunity you might not get for a while. So because you need the money and the experience, you give in to a paltry 2%.

Now the client feels like they own you every minute of your every day. You drop everything to take their calls at all hours of the day, nights, and weekends. All for a paltry 2% commission that you agreed to, which ends up being more like 1.4% or less after all your expenses.

Meanwhile it erodes your confidence, self-esteem, and self-worth. It starts to feel like you're not valuable enough for a "real commission." It's no small wonder why many New Agents quit so soon.

New Agents understand they are still gaining experience. But, you can always raise your fees next time, right?

Nope. Not likely.

What happens instead is you're stuck in a habit of undervaluing yourself. Over time, you allow clients to determine your worth instead of embracing what you believe you're worth and the services you provide.

Listen to a lie long enough and it starts to feel true.

Most agents are poorly prepared for this conversation because they don't know their own value.

Cutting your fees only reinforces compromise and undermines your true value.

Consequently, New Agents end up working for little or no commission and end up quitting too soon because they feel they'll never amount to much in the real estate world.

Your relationship with money

Your sense of self-worth is governed by your relationship with money.

We all have Head Trash. And it devalues self-worth and true value. All your internal garbage surfaces when you have to defend your commission fees.

Believe it or not, most people are uncomfortable with money.

We've all heard of lottery winners who win millions but then lose it all after three years.

(We'd all like to believe we wouldn't let that happen to us, but don't be so sure!)

Much of it is because lottery winners never believed *they* were worth millions. Sudden riches didn't give them the time to grow into a person who is comfortable with money like a true millionaire. A millionaire is simply not *who* they are.

Problems they never had before hit them hard and fast: Old friends become distant because they feel like they're not good enough for them, unknown relatives suddenly surface to "borrow" a few thousand dollars, unscrupulous creditors are coming to collect.

It's a whole new level of life they were never prepared to live because they didn't earn it.

Overnight, they're living in fear, overwhelmed, and alone.

So after three years, the lottery winners unconsciously engages self-destructive behaviors. They're on a spending spree, burning piles of money, and throwing it out the window.

Secretly, they're escaping to their old comfort zone of destitution. Their poverty problems were like old friends, while the new problems with riches terrify them.

Your discomfort with money

It seems strange that people would be uncomfortable with money. But the truth is, we all have our own comfort level, and it is set by our self-image.

For example, ask yourself whether you're worth $1,000 an hour. How about $5,000 an hour?

Can you honestly say you're worth $10,000 an hour?

Your self-image will limit or liberate your comfort level with money. It ultimately determines your ability to earn it. If you think you're worth $50K per year, then that's your (subconsciously self-imposed) limit. You have a set number in your head, and that's what limits you.

For New Agents, it surfaces when you have to defend your commission fees. More often than not, it's too low.

Money, whether you like it or not, reflects your self-perception and self-worth. It is a digital measurement of your value.

But things always feel weird when you have to justify your fees. You don't want to be greedy or needy, but you don't want to appear conceited and over-priced either.

Try this test

As a New Agent, what would you pay yourself to perform the services you offer?

Pick a dollar amount.

Now, compare it to what other agents get. If it's higher, then you're feeling pretty confident.

If it's lower, then you deserve to raise it.

The truth is, you're worth at least as much as the next agent, so don't undersell yourself.

You will always deserve fair market value for your fees.

Top Agents think about money differently

Top Agents know how this works.

If you think you're worth $50,000 then you'll earn $50,000 and no more.

But if you think you're worth $250,000, then you'll do everything you can to prove you're worth $250,000. Or $500,000.

You'll naturally train your mind, plan your days, and work like the kind of agent who deserves a $250,000 income. Even though you may not have it now, you'll grow into it soon enough as you think and behave like a Top Agent.

With consistent practice, don't be surprised when you're cashing $50,000 commission checks!

Over time, the money becomes merely a digit. It's a side-dish reward for delivering extraordinary value to your clients.

As you grow in your negotiation skills, your value jumps dramatically.

But for now, avoid the habit of undervaluing your self-worth...and NEVER undersell yourself!

How to sell yourself and ask for what you're worth

Experienced agents have mastered this skill over time, but New Agents need a script or guideline to follow. A script makes sure you cover all the most important points and allows you to guide the conversation toward a satisfying outcome.

Following this outline will cover the most important points in the right order and guide you to the best outcome possible. You're going show them how you're going to deliver on your promises and what they can expect from you.

Before you begin, have a number set in your mind for your commission. Don't budge.

Now, to build your script, write out and answer these questions for each step. Do this before you meet with your client.

Step 1: Their problems

What were their three greatest problems in selling or buying their property? Why did they call you?

Bring up their problems and pains in selling/buying their property. Remind them why they called you.

Step 2: The solution

What are your solutions for their three biggest problems?

How soon will you implement and solve these problems?

When do you expect it to be done?

What results will your promise to them?

Show them your solutions, and what you will do for them.

Step 3: Your credibility

What similar problems have you solved for past clients?

What have other clients said about working with you?

What do other real estate agents charge for their commissions?

How does it compare to your fees?

Show them what you've done for other clients who are in their situation. Show them other real estate agents' commission fees, and make comparisons.

Step 4: Show them how great things will be when you're done.

What will the outcome look like after the transaction is done? Show. Don't tell.

What problems will be solved?

What is your commission fee?

Show them what their life will look like after the transaction is complete. Paint a detailed picture of much better things will be for them.

Step 5: Anticipate objections and be ready with answers.

What are all their possible objections to you or your solutions? Address their objections before they raise them.

This is the most important part of preparation.

Having answers to *all* their objections *before* they ask immediately earns their confidence in you.

If they ask something you weren't prepared for, you can always respond with, "That's a good question. I'll find the answer and get back to you."

Step 6: Back off and give them space.

When it comes to their money, people value freedom of choice. Give them the option to change. Offer them choices. Advise them to choose the real estate agent who best fits their working style – not the cheapest cost.

If they're still not convinced, graciously walk away. They're not the client you want, because they will likely scrutinize you at every step. And even though they won't say it, they will always think that you are overpaid.

Ideally, you want to work only with the people who appreciate the value of your services.

Refer them to another real estate agent who can "better fit" their needs. But *always* leave them with the option to call you if they change their mind.

The one skill that brings in real cash

Negotiation is something you do the minute you meet a prospective client.

First, you negotiate working together, your commission, and your marketing plan. Then, you negotiate everything with everyone else on behalf of your client.

One Top Agent, Jen, made an excellent point. She said, "If you can't negotiate for your own commission, it's doubtful that you can negotiate well on behalf of your client."

If you must learn just one core skill in this industry, master the art of negotiation.

The good news is you don't have to do this perfectly when you start out.

You can begin with these simple steps:

1. Use the six steps mentioned earlier. Understand the progression and purpose of each step.

2. Sit in on as many closings as you are allowed and watch how it is done by Top Agents.

Negotiation skills are better caught than taught.

3. Follow your mentor closely, as they negotiate with a new client, with other agents, contractors, and even bankers.

Watch for the key elements of communication, especially as they close each stage of the deal: landing a client, negotiating through the transaction, and closing the deal.

Once you get the basics down, the rest comes with practice.

As you improve and grow, your business and income will explode.

Top Agent Success Principle:

If you must learn just one core skill in this industry, master the art of negotiation.

Section II Summary

* Top Agents think about time and money differently, which leads to developing habits that gear them for success. Controlling their calendar naturally controls their income.

* At every stage of their business, Top Agents seek out mentors to help them to the next level.

The most effective mentoring structure has three tiers: mentorees, peer mentors, and career mentors.

* Paying it forward makes you a better, more valuable agent.

* Niche marketing is leaner, more effective, and less risky for a New Agent. It is by far the most cost effective, and efficient approach. Top Agents know their market, while New Agents guess.

* Negotiation is a core skill of every Top Agent.

It is fundamentally the most valuable and lucrative skill successful agents possess at any level.

Now, it's time to answer the most important questions about YOU.

Section III

Will These Principles Work for You?

Top Agents think so. Read on to find out!

Chapter 10

Three Simple Things You Can Do to Launch Your Career

Let's talk about simple actions you can take to move forward.

If you can keep a schedule, keep a promise, and make friends… then you have all you need to get going and keep going.

All great human achievement begins with simple action.

Learn from these Top Agents

Mary Melendez got into real estate as a single mother. She made a promise to her children she would take care of them. So she pursued a career that offered flexible hours to raise her children.

Today, she is a Top Agent and world-class real estate mentor serving in Southern California.

Jennifer Lukus came from corporate America as an executive assistant and project manager for 15+ years. She left that to sell real estate and began by shadowing great agents. Attending open houses to learn from other agents led her to her first listing. In her first month, she got her first sale and sold over $5 million in real deals within her first year.

Becca Berlinsky started when she was in high school, helping a Top Producer at Coldwell Banker. She continued into her college years, and in addition, earned her real estate license and gained valuable experience in the industry. Like most college grads, she wasn't sure what she wanted to do. So she continued full time work in real estate, writing listing contracts, purchase contracts, and everything in between. After the market crashed, she decided to stay with it.

Becca is today a successful agent with her broker's license and enjoys a healthy career in an excellent office. She is contagiously passionate about her work and loves being an Agent.

Jonette Burk got into real estate when she was eight years old. Her parents were real estate brokers, so she often joined them at open houses and showings. When she came of age, she earned her broker's license, and she has worked in escrow, at a title company, as a mortgage broker, and as a real estate agent. She's enjoyed a broad career in the industry and counsels young entrepreneurs to get a good strong start in their businesses.

Each of these agents will tell you the potential for a new life is waiting for you

None of these agents are hyper talented or born into privilege.

They simply set their calendars, kept their promises, made friends, and took action.

Sometimes the wrong action at first, but they knew that if you're not failing, you're not learning.

Through trial and error, they evaluated, course corrected, re-evaluated and grew smarter and stronger. Overtime, success naturally followed.

If Top Agents could speak directly to you, they would all same the same thing: if *they* can do it, so can *you*. No secret formulas, no magic bullets. Just smart work on the right things.

You picked up this book for a reason

If you've read this far, I believe deep down you can do this.

I believe you are called to be an agent.

But if you're doubting that right now, then let's revisit the three questions I set out to answer, what I discovered, and why I think you can make it.

1. Why do some agents make it, while most fail?

Lingering Head Trash and Toxic Beliefs will kill the careers of more than 80% of New Agents this year. Eight out of ten agents who learn the same material from the same trainer will not process it the same way. Head Trash and Toxic Beliefs block their ability to take action on new information, even if that information is good for them. The agents who make it in the business reversed their Toxic Beliefs, and replaced them with empowering beliefs.

Take inventory of your harmful beliefs and begin the process of reversing them.

Then, embrace the beliefs that liberate you and inspire you to take positive action.

2. What are the traits of successful agents? How do they think, and what do they do when they're tempted to quit?

Successful agents develop and practice one simple habit: they keep their promises – to themselves, their clients, and their mentor.

The habit of keeping a dozen tiny promises everyday leads to keeping bigger promises throughout your career. Breaking even the smallest promises, especially with yourself, leads to quitting too soon.

When Top Agents are tempted to quit, they pause and review their promises.

Then they re-commit to keeping their promises to themselves and those around them.

Begin your career the right way by making a list of small, realistic promises and make a commitment to keeping them. It makes it easier to keep bigger promises later.

3. Can you acquire the traits of a successful agent and apply them for your own success?

Absolutely!

These core, success principles are available to anyone.

It requires no special skills to adopt a new habit, make a new friend, or make a promise and keep it.

The principles listed in this book simply give focus to your efforts, and a way to track your progress. You'll know what to do and course correct when needed.

Commit to practicing at least one principle each week.

It will position you for success better than most New Agents this year.

But there is a greater reason why I wrote this book

We MUST dramatically reduce the risk of building your real estate business.

Most New Agents this year will learn a harder and costlier way to build their business. Unfortunately, they will follow the conventional wisdom of the market which leads them to running out of money and quitting too soon.

Your unique creativity and resourcefulness is a powerful hedge against high risk. The real "money" is inside your head.

Angie Weeks didn't have much money to begin her real estate career. So she used her time and talent. She took personal inventory, then leveraged her skills with social media and patiently and steadily built relationships. She trained herself to watch for opportunities to do good, and applied the principles practiced by Top Agents. She is now a Top Agent serving in Orange County, California.

Mary Melendez, a Top Agent we mentioned earlier, has never paid for a lead her entire career.

She uses the phone, walks neighborhoods and talks to people. If you ask her how she does it, she'll tell you that she doesn't sell real estate. She simply makes friends out of strangers.

You don't have to risk a lot of time and money to get started.

To be sure, starting any business is risky. Real estate is no exception. But if you start thinking like a Top Agent, you can safely begin building a fulfilling and lucrative career in real estate.

Try a new career risk free!

It's time to set you on the fast track.

Whether you're brand new to the business, or you're struggling to stay in, there are three things you can do right now.

Taking action on these three things will bring clarity to your goals, restore your confidence and re-ignite your momentum.

1. Meet with your mentor.

Call and set an appointment now. If you don't have a mentor, call the next best agent. The point is, you must reach out if you want to make it in real estate. Your success is heavily dependent on your ability to make friends, so it's best you start practicing now.

When you meet, keep it simple and limit it to an hour. Talk specifically about where you are at the moment, and where you want to be. Then come up with three action steps, and set due dates on when you will complete them. That will make your time together productive, and keep you moving forward.

Read Chapter 5 again. It covers mentors and mentoring in greater detail.

2. Start a journal and share it.

In your journal, answer this one important question: WHY are you a real estate agent?

Keep writing until you gain clarity, and it resonates with your spirit. If it doesn't come clear, pick it up again on your next reflective session. Journaling is important because it forces you to articulate your beliefs in writing. You can untangle twisted thoughts before they rot into Head Trash and clear your mind to install empowering beliefs.

Clarity in your beliefs, ethics and reason for being an agent is a powerful force. It gives direction and purpose to everything you will do as an agent. Most importantly, it establishes your message to those who will do business with you – defining what you will do for the benefit of your clients.

You cannot hold a belief in something you don't clearly understand. And if you don't believe in WHY you do what you do, neither will your potential clients believe in you

Take the time to develop a habit of journaling. Use the protected time to nourish you heart, mind and soul. It promises to be the ten most productive minutes of your day.

Share your journal at your next meeting with your mentor. A good mentor will help you gain the clarity you need to move forward.

Review Chapter 2 to understand the value and purpose of self-reflection.

3. Set a schedule and promise to yourself that you will keep it.

Find your calendar and set schedules, deadlines and promises. Nothing gets done without a deadline.

Set protected, uninterrupted time to journal first thing in the morning, or before you sleep.

Also, set one hour to meet with your mentor each week. A good mentor will plot your next steps and help you set your activity calendar.

Then put your promise in writing, and promise your mentor you will keep it.

Time management is the first habit Top Agents develop, and practice every day. The sooner you embrace this habit, the sooner you'll find your way to success.

Read Chapter 4 again. If time is money, then your new job is to convert time into money.

Is it right for you? Test your career readiness in 21 days

These three quick start action steps are all you'll need to begin your journey – or get you back on track toward a successful real estate career. Anyone can do these right now.

In fact, these three steps should be the first things you do if you're exploring a career in real estate. Meeting with a mentor, keeping a journal and setting a schedule will show you if you're ready to build your own real estate business.

If you can form these habits in 21 days, then you're on the right track. But if you failed to make it to 21 days, then try again until you are successful.

Successful agents know that failing fast and learning fast is the quickest road to success.

These three simple habits cost you nothing compared to the costs of real estate classes, exams, marketing materials, and broker's fees.

Doing these three things is a simple and ultra-low risk way to test your motivation and commitment.

Take 21 days to test if you're personally ready. It might be the best 21 days you've ever spent exploring your future – *virtually risk free.*

Why 21 days? Behavioral experts tell us that it takes 21 days to form a habit. Forming the right habits for success begins with a mentor, a journal and a calendar.

It is by far the most cost effective and risk free way to begin your career.

Chapter 11

Discover Your Unique Genius

Once you have firmly adopted the habits of a Top Agent, congratulations!

You now should have some confidence to move forward.

Let's build on that.

The next step is to form your marketing strategy.

Your challenge is to do it with little or no money.

To minimize your risk, here's how you can achieve that.

Find your unique marketing style

Some agents walk into a crowded room and see strangers as new friends. They bounce through the room starting new conversations, exchanging business cards, collecting phone numbers and leave with a book full of potential clients.

Other agents walk into crowded room and look for at least one person they know. They typically cling to a small circle of people, and rarely venture out.

It's awkward and uncomfortable for them to start face to face conversations. But they're perfectly fine on Facebook, LinkedIn, and Twitter. And that's how *they* build a book full of potential clients.

Every successful agent has their own unique marketing style. Finding clients seems so effortless for them, and we're always hearing about how many escrows they closed last month.

Most of them discovered their marketing style by exploration and experiment, sometimes at great cost.

This is when most New Agents jump into high dollar seminars and buy big budget marketing tools. Many become "Seminar Junkies" and end up as perpetual students in search of their unique marketing style.

At this point, most New Agents are stuck and haven't taken action.

When the credit cards are maxed, they end up feeling frustrated, unproductive, and guilty over wasted days, lost income, lost opportunities, and more debt.

As the money trickles dry, they learn the expensive way that Zillow is not a marketing strategy.

It is a tool.

An effective strategy begins with you

New Agents are willing to spend big bucks on high dollar seminars because they're hoping to find their marketing strategy.

The problem is, no one can determine that for you. This is your business, and your budget.

It gets expensive buying and trying everything until you find a system that works for you.

This approach relies on guesswork and wishful thinking. Guesswork is what most New Agents do in the absence of a real strategy.

But there is a simpler, powerful and affordable way to find what works for you.

We can eliminate the guesswork, get you unstuck, inspire your creativity, leverage your natural talents, and exploit your strengths to build your business.

Strengths-based coaching

If you haven't realized it yet, you have your own unique way of making friends.

In my coaching sessions, I counsel Newbie Startups toward a strengths-based approach to building their business and marketing strategy. It eliminates costly guesswork.

We focus on WHO you are, and HOW you are wired. We work *with* your strengths, not against them.

So if you're an introvert, we won't make you attend large networking parties. And if you're an extrovert, we won't trap you into long, one-on-one conversations.

Our goal is to focus your time and money on methods consistent with your personality, talents and strengths. We recognize your weaknesses, and work with them only to the point they won't undermine your strengths.

And then we exploit your strengths to be the best you can be with who you are and what you have.

Strengths-based coaching begins with taking a strengths assessment inventory, which creates a profile of your five greatest strengths. Then we use your strength profile to design your unique marketing strategy.

With an assessment test, we greatly increase your chances of a building a successful business.

If you're not familiar with Clifton StrengthsFinders, it's time to discover your strengths profile now. It's a small $15.00 and 90-minute investment in you, and the returns are phenomenal.

Learn more here: https://www.gallupstrengthscenter.com/ Home/en-US/Index

Then, go to work on forming your marketing strategy consistent with your strengths. With your strengths profile, you can eliminate marketing methods that don't fit you.

For example, if your dominant strengths include Activator and Communication, you will likely be comfortable in front of large audiences. But if your dominant strengths include Connectedness and Relator, you're probably more comfortable meeting clients one at a time.

Investing in YOU pays the highest dividends

I believe you are your single-most, greatest untapped resource. Your unique natural talents, strengths, and creativity offer you unlimited potential to achieving anything you pursue, and break down barriers blocking your way.

Your most valuable asset will always be YOU. And your most valuable skills are your abilities to learn and solve problems.

That's why we start on building *you* first – not your marketing funnel, email campaign, or social media strategy.

We understand your business will grow only as much as you do, and we believe shaping your heart and mind to serve clients in your unique way leads to a healthy and fulfilling career.

Becoming a Top Agent

Becoming a Top Agent can be summed up in mastering your mindset, resources and relationships.

Then it's assessing your strengths and discovering your unique way of making friends, i.e., your marketing style.

We start with your mind set because it's where you'll encounter the most roadblocks. When you find the truth in your life, you'll move forward with clarity and confidence in who you are and what you believe. Once you are clear on your beliefs, you are unstoppable.

Then we work on practical matters like the relationship between your time and money. If you were ever once an employee, you can't cruise on autopilot to make an income. As an entrepreneur, your new job is to convert your time into money.

It's the only way to successfully transition into a lifestyle where you own your calendar, and your earning potential is virtually limitless. You can truly get out what you put into this business.

Remember, nothing ever happens without a deadline and taking action.

Top Agents set dates, take action, and sometimes make mistakes. When they do, they evaluate, pivot or change course – but they never stop.

If you're not failing, you're not learning. And if you're not learning, you're not growing.

Go forth and blunder boldly, and remember everything in this business is fixable.

The solutions are often a phone call away.

Why I believe in you

There are four reasons why I believe in you.

1. I believe everyone has unlimited, untapped potential.

Most of your abilities, talents and strengths you have today were discovered. At one time they were untapped potential. As you learned and grew, you discovered other talents you never thought you had. Throughout the rest your life time, you will uncover even more as opportunities present themselves. Your imagination is your only limit.

2. I believe everyone is naturally gifted with curiosity and the ability to learn.

You are gifted with a natural ability to solve problems. Puzzles, problems, and mysteries trigger our desire for answers and resolution. Then we learn, improve and grow – always in search of a better way and a higher quality of life.

3. I believe every person has unique, intrinsic value.

You are wired together like no one else. No one else thinks exactly like you or processes life the same way. Your creator even gave you a unique set of finger prints to remind you! You offer a unique contribution to the world in your lifetime and in this generation.

4. I believe everyone is entitled to pursue a quality of life of their choosing.

Because of the first three beliefs, I believe you have the power to choose a life style you love. Use your imagination and dream. Then learn all you can, and be the first to take action by paying it forward.

The one, priceless quality of a Top Agent

Every Top Agent interviewed embodied one enduring, priceless quality: They seek and cherish wisdom and pursue it at all costs. It's part of their DNA, and a key to their success.

So congratulations on reading this far!

May this be your first step among many in your search for priceless wisdom that offers you a quality of life full of love, peace, and prosperity.

I love those who love me [Wisdom], and those who seek me find me.

With me are riches and honor, enduring wealth and prosperity.

My fruit is better than fine gold; what I yield surpasses choice silver.

~ The Proverbs of King Solomon

We've only scratched the surface!

It wasn't possible to capture 276+ years of wisdom, hours of interviews, and months of research and cram it all into this book.

Although there is plenty here to get you started, these principles will take a lifetime to master.

Practicing them daily will shape your professional destiny as a Top Agent.

All Top Agents return to these principles regularly throughout their entire careers, because they know they form a solid foundation for a thriving business.

Although the *methods* to achieving success constantly change, the *principles* for success will always remain the same.

Because you are a dynamic, growing and changing person, make these principles your life's quest as you pursue a career in real estate.

They will serve you well as the foundation for your health and prosperity.

If you're in a Crisis of Meaning, embrace this short episode in your career. Let this book help you get back to basics, and guide you through your journey. Clarity and purpose will become evident when you persevere.

Real wisdom is better caught than taught. Stick around the right people, and everything becomes effortless. You have everything you need to be a Top Agent.

With this book in hand, I believe you can do it, and I know Top Agents who would tell you they believe in you, too.

I wish you all the best.

Here's to your personal growth and success in all you pursue!

E. Theodore Aranda

ABOUT THE AUTHOR

E. Theodore Aranda ("Ed") is a freelance author, business coach and marketing strategist.

He loves assisting New Agents and lean startups launch their businesses.

Ed is also a real estate investor, with specialized training in Ultra Lean Marketing, Business Creation, Customer Value Optimization, Entrepreneurship, Tax and Asset Protection, Creative Financing, Wholesaling, Lease Options, Tax Lien and Deeds, and Probate Properties. He's even bought and sold his own property.

Personal Note

"I believe every New Agent deserves to have the best opportunities for success.

As you read "Winning Secrets...", I hope you gain a fresh perspective on building your real estate career in the fastest, leanest way possible, with immediate and lasting results.

I'm excited for the opportunities before you! As you become a better agent each day, you'll enjoy a rich and fulfilling lifestyle in your new career – on your way up and when you reach the top. Investing in yourself first always yields your greatest returns."

~ Ed

Made in the USA
Middletown, DE
15 January 2020